Laurinda

A NEW PLAY BY

Diana Nguyen

WITH **Petra Kalive**

BASED ON THE NOVEL BY **Alice Pung**

CURRENCY PRESS
The performing arts publisher

NEXTSTAGE | MTC MELBOURNE THEATRE COMPANY

CURRENT THEATRE SERIES

First published in 2022
by Currency Press Pty Ltd,
PO Box 2287, Strawberry Hills, NSW, 2012, Australia
enquiries@currency.com.au
www.currency.com.au

in association with Melbourne Theatre Company

Typeset by Brighton Gray for Currency Press.
Cover features Ngoc Phan (left) and Gemma Chua-Tran.
Cover image by Brett Boardman.

Currency Press acknowledges the Traditional Owners of the Country on which
we live and work. We pay our respects to all Aboriginal and Torres Strait
Islander Elders, past and present.

NATIONAL LIBRARY OF AUSTRALIA

A catalogue record for this
book is available from the
National Library of Australia

Contents

ACKNOWLEDGEMENTS

We acknowledge that this script was written on the lands of the Yalukit Willam Peoples of the Boon Wurrung and Wurundjeri Peoples of the Kulin Nation. We feel privileged to be able to continue a legacy of storytelling on these lands where story, dance and song were integral to culture and understanding the world.

Our biggest thanks go to Alice Pung for entrusting us with this story to share with a whole new generation.

We are indebted to the people who have helped us shape this story along the way: Alice Pung, Brett Sheehy, Chris Mead, Jennifer Medway, Jeremy Rice, Karin Farrell, Janine Snape, Carmen Lai, Fiona Choi, David Lam, Katie Long, Chi Nguyen, Ngoc Phan, Joanne Nguyen, Dean Bryant, Charlotte Nicdao, Jenny Zhou, Eugyeene Teh, Xanthe Beesley, Marco Cher-Gibard, Karine Larché, Rachel Lee, Roshelle Fong, Taylor Fong, Michele Lee, Chi Vu, Merlynn Tong, HaiHa Le, Georgina Naidu, Jillian Nguyen, Ann Truong, Cheryl Ho, Jing-Xuan Chan, Max Brown, Gemma Chua-Tran and Roy Phung.

Laurinda was first produced by Melbourne Theatre Company at Southbank Theatre, the Sumner, Melbourne on 6 August 2022 with the following cast:

KATIE / MRS LESLIE / AS CAST	Fiona Choi
LINH / BRODIE	Gemma Chua-Tran
TRISHA / MRS GREY / MS WHITE / AS CAST	Georgina Naidu
MUM / AMBER / CHARLOTTE / AS CAST	Chi Nguyen
LUCY / LUCY 37	Ngoc Phan
DAD / DR VANDERWERP / AS CAST	Roy Phung
TULLY / CHELSEA / MRS NEWBERRY / AS CAST	Jenny Zhou

Author, Alice Pung
Writer, Diana Nguyen
Writer and director, Petra Kalive
Set designer and AV concept and design, Eugyeene Teh
Costume designer, Karine Larché
Lighting designer, Rachel Lee
Composer and sound designer, Marco Cher-Gibard
AV designer, Justin Gardam
Movement director, Xanthe Beesley
Assistant director and AV composition, Roshelle Fong
Cultural consultant, Alice Qin
Voice and dialect coach, Mark Wong
Vietnamese dialogue, Chi Nguyen

NEXTSTAGE

With a $4.6 million investment by MTC and MTC's Playwrights Giving Circle, the NEXT STAGE Writers' Program has introduced the most rigorous playwright commissioning and development process ever undertaken by the Company, setting a new benchmark for play development in Australia.

Thank you to MTC's Playwrights Giving Circle — its donors, foundations and organisations — for sharing our passion and commitment to Australian stories and Australian writers.

Louise Myer and Martyn Myer AO, Maureen Wheeler AO and Tony Wheeler AO, Christine Brown Bequest, Allan Myers AC QC and Maria Myers AC, Tony Burgess and Janine Burgess, Dr Andrew McAliece and Dr Richard Simmie, Larry Kamener and Petra Kamener

The Ian Potter Foundation

NAOMI MILGROM FOUNDATION

THE MYER FOUNDATION

MALCOLM ROBERTSON FOUNDATION

THE UNIVERSITY OF MELBOURNE

Diana Nguyen   Petra Kalive

DIANA NGUYEN graduated from Monash University in 2005, majoring in Drama and Theatre. Since then her career has evolved into that of being an actor, writer, comedian and producer, and in 2021 she was awarded the Overall Top 40 Under 40 Asian Australian Leadership Award. Her writing credits include her comedy standup shows, *5 Ways to Disappoint Your Vietnamese Mother* in the anthology *Growing up Asian in Australia*, edited by Alice Pung, and the award-winning web series *Phi and Me*, which won a Best International Narrative accolade at New Zealand Webfest. Subsequent to this, the upcoming TV series *Phi and Me* (Northern Pictures) is currently in development with Screen Australia. Diana has also appeared on *Q+A* (ABC), *The Project* (Network 10) and featured in acting roles include the award-winning role of Kim Huong in *Phi and Me* (Sicily webfest); *Tunnel Rat* (Malthouse Theatre); *Viet Kieu* (Melbourne Fringe); *How to Stay Married* (Network 10) and more. Diana is passionate about improvisation and participates with the Melbourne ensemble companies the Humour Foundation and Melbourne Playback Theatre Company. You can listen to Diana on comedy interview podcast *The SnortCast*.

PETRA KALIVE is Associate Director at Melbourne Theatre Company and has previously directed *Touching the Void*, *The Lifespan of a Fact*, *Sexual Misconduct of the Middle Classes* (Green Room Award nominated Outstanding Direction and Outstanding Production), *Hungry Ghosts* and *Melbourne Talam* (Green Room Award-nominated Best Director) for MTC, as well as *Pandora* for MTC NOW. She has also worked for Belvoir Street

Theatre, Sydney Theatre Company, Arena Theatre Company, Complete Works Theatre Company, St Martins Youth Arts Centre, Monash University Centre for Theatre and Performance, La Trobe Performing Arts Department and the Victorian College of the Arts. Independent directorial credits include: *Taxithi* (fortyfivedownstairs, Green Room Award-nominated Best Director); *Oil Babies*, which she also wrote (Lab Kelpie, shortlisted for the NSW Premier's Literary Awards); and *My Brilliant Career*, a musical adaptation by Dean Bryant and Matthew Frank of the Miles Franklin novel (Monash University). Petra was Artistic Director of Union House Theatre from 2014–2019.

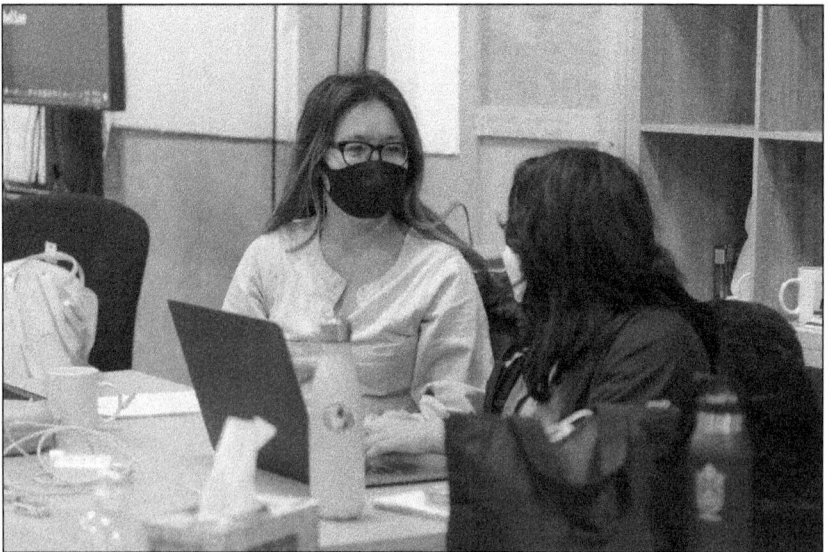

Diana Nguyen (left) and Petra Kalive in rehearsals for the Melbourne Theatre Company production of Laurinda. *Photo: Sarah Walker.*

Foreword

Laurinda had been sitting on the shelf for a while at Melbourne Theatre Company. While several people had wanted to realise it, for some reason it hadn't happened. Then, the first Melbourne lockdown hit in 2020 and, being new to the company with the energy for something to sink her teeth into, Petra grabbed it with both hands. Diana immediately popped into her mind as a collaborator on this work—there was a sensibility to Diana's humour and perspective that Petra thought married well with the essence of Alice's novel. Diana's work had also featured in Alice's anthology *Growing Up Asian in Australia*—and we were both huge fans of Alice's writing.

We had worked together years previously in an improvisational company and knew our values centred around collaboration, the advancing and extending of offers, deep listening, the use of metaphor, the drive to find the 'heart' of a moment, and the humour—always humour.

So, during that first lockdown, we began developing this work over Zoom (and sometimes phone when the internet connection was dodgy) and had a series of workshops (live and virtual) with actors. These workshops were invaluable. Developing the work with the support of so many Asian-Australian actors and creatives has made the work what it is. We could not have articulated the nuance of experience, nor been so bold, without their challenges and generosity. We thank them from the very bottom of our hearts.

We could not be more grateful to Alice Pung. Not only for her trust in us to translate her coming-of-age story but also for her generosity in the way she has allowed us to adapt the work so it speaks to a whole new audience. While so many reviews of the book categorise *Laurinda* as 'charming', 'relatable', 'important' and 'insightful', what sits underneath their positive statements is a diminishing of the power of what we have uncovered through Alice's work. She has written an honest, uncomfortable and exposing investigation of the negotiation necessary to walk between cultures. She effortlessly and with humour communicates the internal trauma that is carried intergenerationally

Clockwise from front left: Chi Nguyen, Ngoc Phan, Roy Phung, Gemma Chua-Tran and Jenny Zhou in rehearsals for the Melbourne Theatre Company production of Laurinda. *Photo: Sarah Walker.*

and the strength and self-love that is required to simply exist. The magnificence of what Alice has achieved is that she makes this complex and difficult existence relatable and charming, important and insightful, while exposing structural, casual and internalised racism. Perhaps her book was ahead of its time. Although set in a high school, what was clear to us from the beginning was that this was a coming-of-age story that isn't only experienced at fifteen years old. It is coming-of-age for every age because reconciling the constant and unrelenting negotiation that the dominant (white) culture demands is unceasing.

So we decided to set *Laurinda* deliberately in 1997 and 2021—two periods of intense and visible Asian-hate in Australia. In 1997, Pauline Hanson formed the One Nation Party and her maiden speech railed against Indigenous rights, so-called 'political correctness' and 'reverse-racism', and called for the halting of migration to Australia because she feared that Australia was being 'swamped by Asians'. She contributed to shaping the cultural conversation about racism and normalising xenophobia. In 2020, with the arrival of Covid-19, like many other parts of the world, anti-Asian hate crime soared, following news that the virus originated in Wuhan, China. While in the intervening years, conversation about Asian-focused racism was not front and centre, what the coronavirus event demonstrated was how close to the surface the racist sentiment was in Australia. It revealed how much work there is still to do. While we were experiencing the real-life events of 2020, it was impossible to interrogate a book set prior to the advent of Google and not engage with complex conversations about how far we've come as a society, how far we have still to go and where the pressure points are on the individual who experiences prejudice, bigotry, and bias. It is for this reason that we made the character of Lucy begin the play as a woman in her late 30s, living today, reliving her fifteen-year-old self through the lens of her adulthood. We took inspiration from the coming-of-age classic *Freaky Friday*. Lucy is transformed into her own body, 25 years younger. This form allows us to stay true to the comedy and light touch of Alice Pung's novel, but layers in a dramatic tension that gives the play momentum.

We also deliberately centralised this family home of Vietnamese refugees. We both have lived experience of growing up second-generation Australians and felt it was important to articulate the specific pressures on a young Vietnamese-Australian woman. It was very important for Diana to see a production on the mainstage articulate the nuance of a refugee family fleeing war for a better life. We would like to thank Chi Nguyen for her Vietnamese translation, which we feel really grounds this family arc of the story and authentically communicates a Vietnamese sensibility.

Returning to the 1990s allowed us to revel in nineties music. We have had the best time reliving our teenage years and injecting the play with references you will only get if you lived it. Relooking at the 1990s through a post-2020 lens offers the opportunity to play, reframe, cringe and laugh at what we were, to better understand where we find ourselves today.

What we have endeavoured to do in adapting *Laurinda* is reveal current ideas about representation and appropriation, and deep dive into who gets to tell what stories. We know that the stories that we tell have a cultural 'ripple effect'. Alice Pung's novel has already made significant impact. We hope that by adapting it for the stage, we continue the conversation she started with a whole new audience. We hope to improve connection, empathy and understanding, and if we're lucky generate discussion and debate about where we are headed as a culture.

A big thank you to MTC's NEXT STAGE program. We couldn't have done it without the support. We need ongoing investment in Australian stories and storytellers, so that the cultural identity on our stages is as rich and complex as the Australia we live in.

Big love. And thank you.

Diana and Petra

CHARACTERS

LUCY, 15 years old. Year 10, model Asian.

LUCY 37, 37 years old. Teacher, model Asian—Lucy can be heard by everyone.

LINH, only the audience and Lucy can hear Linh.

Stanley

MUM, Quyen Thi Lam, doesn't feel confident speaking English.

DAD, Hung Lam, wants success for his daughter.

TULLY, has more As than a box of batteries. Eyes like small desperate fires.

CHARLOTTE, student 2021.

Laurinda

The Cabinet—students who rule the school:

BRODIE, a natural leader—steely, ambitious, competitive, but desperate to be seen as 'good'.

AMBER, wants to be seen.

CHELSEA, trying to keep it cool, when all she wants to do is scream.

Teachers

MRS GREY, principal—don't mess with her.

DR VANDERWERP, young History teacher, brilliant mind.

MRS LESLIE, Amber's mum, Literacy Coordinator, Asian obsession.

Students

KATIE, talks a mile a minute, honest to a fault.

TRISHA, genius pianist, great ears.

From left: Petra Kalive, Chi Nguyen, Fiona Choi, Ngoc Phan, Xanthe Beesley, Jenny Zhou, and Roy Phung in rehearsals for the Melbourne Theatre Company production of Laurinda. *Photo: Sarah Walker.*

The Cabinet's mothers

MRS WHITE, Chelsea's mum—age has been cruel, wine helps.

MRS NEWBERRY, Brodie's mum—does 'good', doesn't suffer fools, will always play for power.

NOTES

All roles should be cast with actors of colour.

Lucy, Linh, Mum and Dad are of Vietnamese heritage. Dad is Teochew.

Can be played with a cast of 7 (6F/1M)

Scenes at home to be spoken in Vietnamese.

/ indicates point of next line beginning

— indicates cut-off line

SETTING

Stanley is a fictional suburb in Melbourne.

Laurinda is an exclusive private girls' school in the inner east of Melbourne.

This is a memory play. Lucy is 37 years old (LUCY 37) and 15 years old (LUCY). The actor playing Lucy needs to play both ages in some scenes. This is indicated by the change in her character designation (LUCY or LUCY 37).

Present time 2021.

Past 1997.

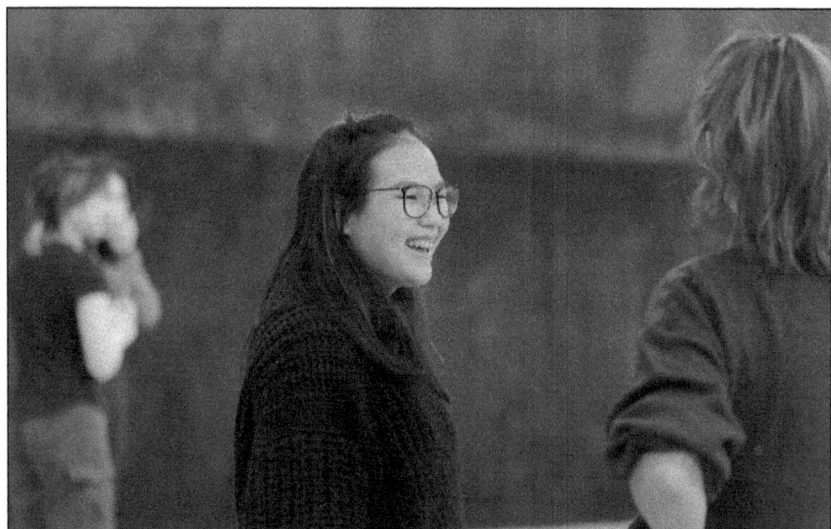

Chi Nguyen in rehearsals for the Melbourne Theatre Company production of Laurinda. *Photo: Sarah Walker.*

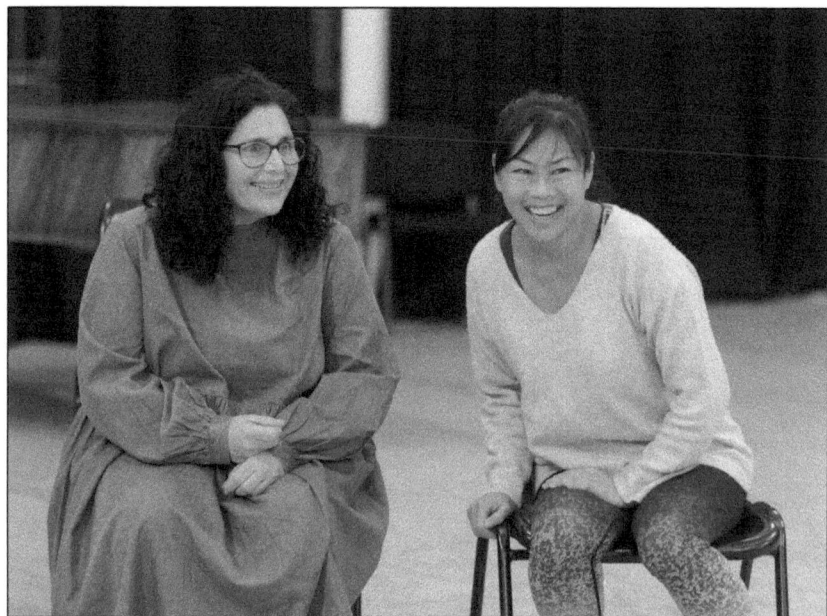

Georgina Naidu (left) and Fiona Choi in rehearsals for the Melbourne Theatre Company production of Laurinda. *Photo: Sarah Walker.*

It is evening.

LUCY 37 *stands at the basin of a school toilet, panicking.*

LUCY 37: Breathe. Breathe.
　　　You're gonna be okay …
　　　Why?! Brodie Newberry? Why??
　　　Calm down Lucy. Calm down.
　　　You got this. Go up there, accept the bloody award. Smile. Make the speech and get on with your life. She probably won't even remember you.
　　　No. I can't do this. I can't do this.
　　　WHY?! Why?? Her?? Of all people.

By this time LUCY 37 *is on the ground in the foetal position, holding her eye.*

There is a call from her dad, which she rejects.

LINH *appears in a banana suit.*

　Not now!

LINH: What are you doing?

LUCY 37: Oh. Crap. Sorry. I didn't realise anyone else was in here.

LINH: Are you okay?

LUCY 37: Yeah … I mean … I'm fine. Just a bit … nervous … I guess … were you here the / whole time?

LINH: Big night. Big speech. Everyone's talking about it.

LUCY 37: Yeah … sorry do I know you?

LINH: [*imitating Gwen Stefani*] This shit is bananas—b a n a n a s. This shit is bananas. / B a n a n a s.

LUCY 37: Okay. So.
　　　You doing something for drama? Is there a performance tonight?

LINH: Nah, I have a friend whose not peeling well, why are you squinting?

LUCY 37: My eye's twitching. What are you—

LINH: Annoying. Nerves. Usually born of paranoia, the need to control.

LUCY 37: Excuse me?

LINH: You know, you have no control over the way people see you.
　　　Like Brodie Newberry.

LUCY 37: I'm not sure I ... ?

LINH: I guess she is the chief justice. Big job. Important. / Powerful. Meaningful work. Such impact.

LUCY 37: I know. I know I know I know I know.

LINH: Aren't they waiting for you?

LUCY 37: I've got some time. They've got a whole video about my teaching career to show first. I do *not* need to watch it. Doesn't feel particularly groundbreaking. I'm just doing my job. Like every other teacher here. Help students feel excited about learning. So embarrassing to sit there with everyone watching. So I thought I'd take a moment. I'm not sure why I'm telling you that.

LINH: Five minutes. That should be enough time.

> LUCY 37*'s phone rings.*

LUCY 37: Um.

> This has been great, but I'm gonna, I should probably ... this has been ... weird.

> [*Answering the phone*] Hi. *Khong khong khong.* Yeah I can. How's Mum? I know. Yup. I've got her stuff in the car. I have to do this speech thing and then ... Dad, don't stress me out okay. I know—I'll be there soon. They're taking good care of her aren't they? ... Okay. Toothbrush! Okay! I'll get it. Bye.

LINH: Everything okay?

LUCY 37: Fine. Sorry. Are you in my Year Ten literature class? Sorry it's hard to tell, through the ...

LINH: I know you. You know me.

LUCY 37: [*realising*] Oh no, it's you!

LINH: Tada ...

LUCY 37: How did you?

> I'm ... oh my God ... I'm having a psychological breakdown minutes before one of the biggest ... Great. So great. Of course ... it's you ... now ... why?!

> LUCY 37 *squeezes her eyes shut.*

Breathe. Lucy. You're okay. Breathe. You can just leave now and get on with your mediocre life. Linh is not here. She's not here. She's not here.

> LUCY 37 *opens her eyes.*

You're still here.

LINH: You're not mediocre.

LUCY 37: I don't …

LINH: You're award winning.

LUCY 37: Mum's in hospital. I have to give a speech in what? Five minutes? I have a bunch of students who I need to … I can't be everything, let alone B-two to your B-one!

LINH: I have a spare suit.

LUCY 37: No no no.

LINH: *We have to do this now.*

LUCY 37: This isn't the right time.

LINH: We can't miss this opportunity.

LUCY 37: Piss off. This is none of your business.

LINH: You've been good. So good. Such a good teacher. Such a good person. Good. Good good good good good good. But you're better than good. You can show you how to do it better.

LUCY 37: I'm fine. Thank you.

LINH: No you're not. I just found you on the floor in the foetal position. So she became the youngest chief justice in the history of chief justices and you became a teacher. So what?

LUCY 37: She … I … I mean.

LINH: You need to go back to go forward.

LUCY 37: I will go back out there—just give me a few minutes.

LINH: That's all we need. To go back to school.

LUCY 37: Linh. I don't have time for this.

LINH: Actually you do. You ready to go back to Laurinda?!

> LINH *clicks and suddenly* LUCY 37 *can't move. 'Pump Up the Jam' begins softly …*

LUCY 37: What? I don't … Oh my God! I. CAN'T. MOVE. I'm having a stroke.

LINH: No you're not. Just stop blinking—leave your eyes open. OPEN YOUR EYES!!

LUCY 37: What is happening? My legs.

LINH: Calm down. You're okay. I mean you're not okay, you kicked me out of your life. But it's time to sort that mess out. We're going back to the nineties.

LUCY 37: I don't want to do that. I don't understand / what's happening?

LINH: It's now or never Lucy Lam. I can't watch you like this anymore!

LUCY 37: I really am going bananas.

LINH: Nah, that happened a long time ago. We're just picking up some much needed advice from a very smart fifteen-year-old. In the nineties!

> LINH *sings along to 'Pump Up the Jam'.*

LUCY 37: Why?

LINH: I'm actually pumped. This is gonna be fun, remember the nineties, how / you would—

LUCY 37: I am dying.

> LINH *slaps or zaps* LUCY 37.

LINH: Stop. Seriously. Shut up and listen for once. If we don't do this, you're never gonna be happy. This needs to happen NOW.

LUCY 37: Nah nah nah / nah nah.

LINH: You are remembering—the / bus …

LUCY 37: There's so much I haven't done.

LINH: My point exactly. The four-oh-six bus. The Victory Carpet Factory? Travelling through Sunray to Stanley? Remember?

> *The world begins to shift.*

LUCY 37: Holy shit, what is happening?

LINH: We're remembering Stanley—the strip of seven shops. Covered in graffiti?

LUCY 37: Everything is moving?!

LINH: Would you just calm down!

> The milk bar! With faded packets of instant noodles and tins of soup. Samboy chips, Red Skins, Seven-Ups.

LUCY 37: Stanley?

LINH: Just go with it. Stanley Spirits. Busiest shop in the strip. Famous for its VB—like most men in the area—bitter.

LUCY 37: Can you smell that?

LINH: That's right! Stanley. Wet cardboard. / Overripe fruit—

LUCY 37: Diesel. Yeah. I can smell that!

LINH: Good. You lived in the only blue house in Stanley—

LUCY 37: Yeah a blue house full of boxes—floor to ceiling of fabric and the latest fast-fashion. Why do I feel like I'm there?

LINH: You loved how it stood out; it was the kind of house a kid would draw, a rectangle in blue and a triangle in red.

> LINH *conjures* DAD *looking at the fruit tree.*

LUCY 37: Dad?

LINH: Dad's watering the plum tree at the front.

DAD: *Tưới làm gì cho tốn nước.* Rain will water tree. (It's a waste of water. Let the rain take care of it.)

> MUM *appears at her sewing machine—she is dressed in fluorescent pants, Esprit T-shirt and plastic sandals.*

LUCY 37: Mum?!

LINH: There she is, sewing—Remember she only goes out to shop, collect the mail, or attend church.

MUM: *Làm xong homework đi rồi ra phụ mẹ khâu mấy cái button nha con.* (Finish your homework and come help me with these buttons.)

DAD: *Có đứa nào ném đá qua window trước nhà mình nè.* (They just threw this rock through our front window.)

LUCY 37: They look so young.

LINH: Shhh. They can hear you!

DAD: Where we live is not a place where good stories begin.

LUCY 37: Can they hear you?

LINH: Nope. Listen to this.

> *We hear nineties music and Pauline Hanson's maiden speech, and we are transported to 1997.*

LUCY 37: This is hell, isn't it?

LINH: We're back now. You are fifteen. You are about to be in Year Ten. And you will respond as you did back then. They are the rules.

LUCY 37: Wait. What? What's going on?

LINH: You're gonna relive it—and I'm out—for now! Pouf!

> LINH *disappears.*

LUCY 37: Linh? Hang on a sec. What's happening? Where am I? I don't want to do this!

> *Laurinda appears.* LUCY 37 *unfreezes.*

TULLY: Wooohoooo. So glad that's over. Take that, Laurinda!

> *She gives the building the finger.*

LUCY 37: Tully! Wait, did we just finish the scholarship exam? How did I get here?

TULLY: I know, right? We travelled to zone one for that?

LUCY 37: [*remembering*] Yeah, we did. The city from this perspective. So green.

TULLY: I can't believe it. That was actually so much easier than I thought. It's like I paid for them to have that final question in there. I figured I might get a bonus credit if we knew about Amnesty International and the Universal Declaration of Human Rights. I mean, was that too much? It was one of my practice essays. I remembered as much as I could.

LUCY 37: I've watched you train for this moment your whole life.

TULLY: 'The Equal Access Scholarship for Youth will ensure your child's future.'

LUCY: 'At Laurinda we promise success.'

TULLY: The E.A.S.Y. Scholarship—Easy?! Ha!

LUCY: Nothing EASY about that.

> *Lights shift. Vietnamese SBS radio.* MUM *gives* LUCY *a letter.*
> LUCY *exists in both memories at the same time.*

LUCY 37: What's this?

MUM: *Mẹ không biết.* (I don't know!)

TULLY: You don't need to study, you're just smart.

LUCY: 'Dr Tully Cho—chief heart surgeon at the largest private hospital in Australia!'

TULLY: [*imitating her mother*] 'But not of the world! Wahhhhh my daughter is such a disappointment!'

> *They both laugh.*

Over three hundred students and only one farking spot!

LUCY: [*imitating her mother*] '*Troi oi,* sixty-five bucks down the drain!' (OMG, sixty-five bucks down the drain!)

Promise me whatever happens, nothing changes?

TULLY: Friends for life. But I really really really really really want it and I promise not to look down on you when I get it.

LUCY: Bitch.

TULLY: Scrag.

LUCY: Nerd

TULLY: Oh—you have gone too far! Too far!

> LUCY *and* TULLY *both open their letters ...*

LUCY: EEEEEAAAHHHHHHH. YEAHHHHHHHH—

MUM: *Cái quỷ gì mà con la lên giữ vậy? Khẽ thôi.* Your brother sleeping. (What devil is inside you to make you behave like that? Be quiet. Your brother is sleeping.)

LUCY: I got in.

> LUCY *clicks. They jump up and hug each other.* MUM *tells* LUCY *how proud she is.* LINH *pops out.*

LINH: Cut Cut. Lucy Lam?! Seriously you know this never happened. You can't change history just because it was something you missed. Nup nup. Don't take the mickey out of this!

LUCY 37: This is silly. I don't even know why we're doing this. / Is this a dream?

LINH: Shut up. We're not doing it your way anymore Lucy.

> *Snap back to past reality.* LINH *disappears.* DAD *enters.*

DAD: *Có sao không?* (What's wrong with you?)

MUM: *Nhà mình có một đứa thông minh sáng dạ.* Smartass. (We have a smartass in the family.)

> *Lucy's brother cries,* MUM *leaves huffing.*

> *Thấy chưa, con làm brother thức rồi kìa.* (Now you've woken your brother up!)

LUCY: I got in!

> DAD *grabs the letter from* LUCY *and begins reading it and all the information.* TULLY *is still there, different time / place.*

TULLY: [*to herself—imitating her mother*] 'Your cousin got into a private college seven years ago and there is no way you are stupider than her.'

DAD: I thought that Tully would get in. She works harder than you. Smarter than you too. You know, you have done more schooling than me now.

LUCY: Tully, it should've been you.

MUM: *Hai trăm hai lăm đô? Tui tưởng ông kêu nó được scholarship mà?* (Two hundred and twenty-five dollars? I thought you said she was on scholarship?)

TULLY: Nah. You're super smart.

TULLY *slowly walks away over the following.*

DAD: Two hundred and twenty-five dollars. Only the jacket. *Bà nhìn giá tiền cái váy nè!* (Two hundred and twenty-five dollars. And that's only the jacket. Look at the price of a skirt!)

TULLY: Don't forget about us losers.

MUM: *Đồng phục đắt tiền có làm nó học khôn ra đâu chứ? Để dành tiền cho bốn cái miệng ăn phải hơn không.* I make skirt. (How will an expensive uniform / help her study better? We need that money for the four mouths in this house. I'll make the skirt.)

DAD: *Không được. Cái bà này,* what will the teachers think of this cheapskate family? I will take the extra shift on Sunday. *Con gái ba bây giờ là scholarship girl rồi.* (No. Old woman. What will the teachers think of this cheapskate family? I will take the extra shift on Sunday. She is a scholarship girl now.)

LUCY: I'm really happy at Christ Our Saviour. All my friends are there.

MUM: *Ông thấy chưa? Nó có phải đổi trường đâu. Tiết kiệm được bao nhiêu tiền.* Save money. (See? She doesn't need to go. We can save so much money.)

DAD: Your friends are stupid girls. Except Toolly. Poor girl, *phải học trường công.* (Your friends are stupid girls. Except Toolly. Poor girl stuck in a government school. I always knew you were smarter.)

MUM: Smarter, minus two hundred and twenty-five *đô!* (Smarter—minus two hundred and twenty-five dollars!)

TULLY: I never imagined I'd be the one left behind.

Classical piano plays.

KATIE, *who talks a mile a minute, finds* LUCY.

KATIE: You're new aren't you? It's so obvious. You look kinda lost. And also I can see the packet folds in your shirt and no-one wears a ribbon in Year Ten. Like no-one. Don't worry, you look great. I'll take you to assembly if you like? We just need to follow the music. I'm Katie.

LUCY: Lucy.

KATIE: Where are you from?

LUCY: Melbourne.

KATIE: Yeah, but where were you from?

LUCY: Oh … I went to Christ Our Saviour in Stanley?

KATIE: Oh no, not your old school! I mean, where are you from?

LUCY: Well where are you from?

KATIE: What do you mean? I'm just Australian. Boring.

[*Listening to the music*] She's good, isn't she?

[*Looking around*] Have you had a tour of the school yet?

LUCY: / Um—

KATIE: / Laurinda is one of the oldest ladies' colleges in the state. It is a Christian institution, so like once a term the students attend church. Probably a lot less than your old school—Catholics, right?

The bells in the tower over there were shipped from London in eighteen eighty-six. I love history! There are three campuses. The junior school, Mead Memorial Hall is down the road. This is the middle school, Lovett College, and next year we get to go to the historically significant Arcadia Avenue campus. This is the new Sheehy Performing Arts Centre. Yeah, I'm not a fan of modern architecture but it has heaps of rehearsal rooms for private lessons.

Trisha, the one that's playing Rachmaninov—again—is in this building constantly with the other music nerds working on their 'craft'—so outside class, this is where they'll be, even at lunch. Oh my God, there's so much to tell you. Ha! *So Much to Tell You.* John Marsden. Get it? No? Cool cool. The woggy girls sit eating their smelly food behind the pool. Maths geeks and science dorks kinda hang near the oval—which really annoys the aths girls who are always like running. Like what are they running for? Or to? There are other Asians here too, but unless they win random maths awards, like you kinda forget they're here. They're so quiet.

I wonder where the Cabinet are? Probably orchestrating a prank of some kind. They do that all the time. It's so funny. On the last day of Year Nine, they played a prank on Trisha. She was playing Beethoven in assembly and five minutes later the bell rang! I mean what were we meant to do? It was the last bell for the year. The teachers couldn't stop the students from leaving, and Trisha was in a trance she didn't realise until forty minutes later that everyone had left!

They arrive at assembly and sit down.

LUCY: What's in the Cabinet?

KATIE: Oh my God. Strap yourself in! Brodie, Amber and Chelsea are the Cabinet. Gosh that makes them sound like a toilet. French—*les cabinets*. They would die! He he. This is so cool like I've never had an Asian friend before.

> *As they are announced,* BRODIE, AMBER *and* CHELSEA *appear, haloed by light—they are picture perfect—on display.*

The Cabinet are like a Laurindan tradition. In the eighteen-nineties, Laurinda was a finishing school for young ladies. After the girls were educated they were said to be 'in the Cabinet'—like on display for eligible bachelors. So like gross. But yeah, it's still kinda the same today—beauty, wealth, personality determine your Cabinet position. Brodie's kind of like the leader coz she's sooo smart and soooo funny and soooo pretty. She was amazing as Proctor in *The Crucible*. Like so much better than Daniel Day Lewis. It's so unfair that she's like good at everything. Amber is like a model and her parents are like SUPER rich! Her mum works here—well sort of— and they are like always fighting. And Chelsea—I used to think she was mean, but she's actually kinda cool—she just has RBF … resting bitch face—she was so nice the other day. She's organised for Amber's dad to get my Daniel Johns autograph valued! I love the band Silverchair so much. I've read the book too. I'm obsessed with all things Silverchair. I so didn't expect Chelsea to, you know, like be so generous. Daniel Johns is my life. We have the same birthday, I think it's a sign.

LUCY: I'm guessing that's them.

KATIE: Obviously. Being a part of the Cabinet means you become part of Laurindan legend. Brodie, Amber and Chelsea's mums were all in the Cabinet too! And everyone still talks about that year and the things they did! My mum was in their year too. I don't see her so much anymore. She really didn't want me to come here. I live with my grandma who is like so strict. I never get to go to parties. The Cabinet hold the best parties—with boys. I guess that's why I don't get to go. But it's just one of the ways the Cabinet keep the Laurinda spirit alive.

> *The concerto concludes and* LUCY *enthusiastically applauds. No-one else does. A beat.* TRISHA *stands and takes a bow. No-one ever claps.* TRISHA *exits beaming.*

BRODIE *approaches almost in slow motion—it is* LINH. *She stands at the podium flanked by* CHELSEA *and* AMBER. *She commands the space.* LUCY 37 *is shocked by seeing Brodie inhabited by* LINH.

LUCY 37: Linh?!

Time stops for a moment—only LUCY 37 *and* LINH *can talk.*

LINH: I always wanted to know what it was like to be Brodie. But really, this is a role of a lifetime. And since I'm in control for a change, it's my time to shine. An Asian playing a role other than Asian!

Everything resumes. BRODIE *waits patiently while* LUCY *sits back down and 'plays' fifteen years old again.*

BRODIE: Mrs Grey asked me to speak today as we herald in the new year. For those of you who don't know me I am Brodie Newberry. Thank you Trisha for sharing your talent with us. We hear you so often it is easy to forget how good you are. Laurinda is so lucky to have you.

Today is a very special day for all of us and marks a very exciting chapter for Laurinda as we welcome a *jade stone* to our golden crown. Can we please show our inaugural Equal Access Student, Lucy Lam a warm Laurindan welcome. Lucy—we hope you embrace this investment in you as much as we champion a multicultural and socioeconomically diverse school community. We have so much to offer you.

LINH, *playing Brodie, winks at* LUCY—*there is vibrant applause from the students.*

MRS GREY *raises one hand to shush them, everyone else raises their hands in silence.*

MRS GREY: At Laurinda we pride ourselves on our acts of public service. You are all here because of your natural talent and leadership potential. With our guidance you could be anything—because at Laurinda we promise success.

The air is sucked out of the room. We are suddenly in MRS GREY'*s office.*

The girls have disappeared. An interrogation.

We have never awarded a scholarship to someone from your circumstances and although you were the best amongst your cohort, it is important to understand the subordinate calibre of your previous education. What books did you study last year?

LUCY: *Looking for Alibrandi* by Melina Marchetta.

MRS GREY: Hmmmhuh. We prefer focusing on the classics in the curriculum. Dickens, Austin, the poetry of Donne, Keats—contemporary classics, Graham Greene, Edith Wharton, Fitzgerald.

What does your father do?

LUCY: Dad works at Victory.

MRS GREY: Trading Finance?

LUCY: A carpet factory.

MRS GREY: What about your mother? Home duties?

LUCY *nods.*

Hmmmhuh. Do you speak English at home?

LUCY: Yeah with Dad.

MRS GREY: Yes?

LUCY: What?

MRS GREY: Yes Mrs Grey. But English is a second language. So. As a condition of your scholarship you will participate in a bridging course with Mrs Leslie our Literacy Co-ordinator.

LUCY: But I thought my essay was good?

MRS GREY: Yes. I was surprised by that. I was expecting a maths score would tip you over the line. You were one of two good essays.

LUCY: But mine was better?!

MRS GREY: Fishing for compliments, are we, Ms Lam? The other piece was outstanding. About the founder of Amnesty International.

LUCY: How come you didn't pick her?

MRS GREY: A student who goes to 'cram school' and rote-learns to pass exams does not meet the criteria at Laurinda. We saw promise in your essay—critical thinking, good structure, eloquent—not quite the standard we expect from our girls but it demonstrated … promise. *Concordia prosum, semper progrediens, semper sursum.* Forward harmony always progressing, always aiming high.

A knock on the door.

You may enter.

BRODIE: Excuse me Principal Grey, you asked me to join you after homeroom.

LUCY 37 *waves at* BRODIE / LINH.

BRODIE / LINH: [*whispering*] Stop it.
LUCY 37: I just find all this so weird …
BRODIE / LINH: Just smile.

They both smile and return to playing LUCY *and* BRODIE. *Beat.*

MRS GREY: Ah yes Brodie.

[*To* LUCY] Brodie has generously volunteered as an act of social service to be your mentor and has been apprised of your situation and will support you—as we deem necessary. Here, the girls are engaged in all types of enriching activities—debating, music, theatre, sport—

BRODIE: We do hope you will be able to partake in these activities while you are here.

KATIE *enters the room—she is in the next scene.*

Remember, Socrates Circle, everyone.
LUCY 37: What fifteen-year-old says 'partake'?

The students are unsupervised in the classroom. Each has a piece of paper in front of them. CHELSEA *tears up her piece of paper and drops it on the floor.* BRODIE *and* LUCY *enter the classroom together.*

BRODIE: Oh God there's Katie.
Lucy. You have to sit with us.

LUCY *takes a step to* BRODIE, *but then she looks at* KATIE *and sits with her.*

KATIE: Where were you? Don't worry you're not late. Dr V brought the wrong worksheets to class. He does that.
CHELSEA: Dr *Vandertwerp* is such a limp biscuit. Lucky he's hot!

CHELSEA *sprays herself with Impulse deodorant.*

KATIE: He's a professor of history, expert in Anglo-Saxon England with articles published in some of the most prestigious history journals in the world.

Something unspoken between the Cabinet. KATIE *is their target.*

CHELSEA: 'The most prestigious history / journals in the world.'

AMBER: While compiling glossaries might have been an important activity in Anglo-Saxon England perhaps it's irrelevant for year ten history education. No offence.

CHELSEA: [*rolling up her skirt so it sits mid-thigh*] The question on everyone's lips is, why is such an 'exceptional professor' teaching fifteen-year-olds?

KATIE: Gross.

AMBER: He's inadequate.

BRODIE: You know Amber, Katie didn't even find the history essay last week difficult?

AMBER: What?! But that last page was a trick question.

CHELSEA: Was it? / Really?

KATIE: What / do you mean?

AMBER: Hm mmm. Mum told me Vandertwerp was laughing about it in the staffroom, thinking he'd fooled us.

CHELSEA: Love having your mum on staff Amber! She does such good work helping the remedials.

LUCY: Remedials?

CHELSEA: Yeah, Amber's mum loves teaching the 'basics'. You might have met her? Mrs Leslie?

LUCY: The Literacy Coordinator?

AMBER: She's not on staff. It's voluntary. Gives her something to do with her day.

BRODIE: [*imitating her mother*] 'One must give back.'

AMBER: I wish. Ever since she's come back from China she's more like: 'Talking does not cook rice.' So embarrassing.

> AMBER, BRODIE *and* CHELSEA *look at* LUCY *with a smile—target has shifted.*

CHELSEA: Laaaaaamby. Isn't Amber's mum teaching you?

LUCY: Just call me Lucy. Lucy Lam. There's no b.

CHELSEA: This school is full of sheep, you fit right in. Baaaaa. Lamby. Get it?! Ha.

BRODIE: Chelsea. English is her second language and she's come from a government school on the EASY scholarship, so she's doing remedial English to make sure she's ready for our advanced academic level. [*To* LUCY] Ignore them, we're actually very inclusive here.

KATIE: What was the trick in the question? You're joking, right?

BRODIE: You're such a genius Katie, I'm sure you figured it out.

KATIE: Yeah. Hope you're right. I need straight As if I'm going to even be considered for the Historical Future Leaders Scholarship.

CHELSEA: Typical.

AMBER: I can't even believe that's a thing.

KATIE: Amber … ?

AMBER: Yes. Katie.

KATIE: I'm just dying to see if your dad's friend has looked at Daniel Johns' autograph yet? I hate to ask you, but it's just so precious to me. And like oh my God, have you heard their new single, 'Freak'? It's like so wicked. Oh, and the video clip where they transfer their sweat to an old lady, and she like becomes younger and morphs into an alien. I wish it was me on that surgical bed, like being given Daniel Johns' sweat.

Beat. The Cabinet look at each other and roll their eyes.

DR VANDERWERP *enters with a thermos of tea and fresh photocopies. He coughs with the stench of deodorant spray.*

DR VANDERWERP: Can I request again that we refrain from deodorising in my classroom.

I don't know how that mix-up happened. Now that I have the correct document, if you could please hand the other one back.

LUCY *hands back the paper.*

Oh thank you. Ling … Lean. Am I getting it right?

CHELSEA: Just call her Lucy. She 'prefers' it.

DR VANDERWERP: Chelsea White, why on earth would you tear up the paper and throw it on the floor?

CHELSEA: [*bending over to pick up the paper*] So sorry Dr V—I won't do it again.

As she rises CHELSEA *sneezes deliberately at* DR VANDERWERP's *crotch.* DR VANDERWERP *screams and jumps backward with disgust, almost tripping on a student. The Cabinet giggle.* CHELSEA *slips out of the classroom, unseen by* DR VANDERWERP.

DR VANDERWERP: Some of us might have concerns about spreading illness to others. I will ask again. If you have any illnesses, please refrain from coming to class or at least sneeze into a tissue.

He composes himself with a sip of tea.

Okay. Well. Let's return to the causes of World War One. We'll be studying everything up to the Vietnam War. Lucy! We will be requiring your input. A personal experience always helps bring the past to life.

Everyone looks to LUCY. *Awkward.*

In the meantime, Brodie, you wanted to share your work on the Triple Entente.

LUCY *turns away and finds herself face to face with* TULLY, *who looks different—there's a change in her—a sharpness.*

TULLY: What is it like?

LUCY: What?

TULLY: Laurinda, dickhead.

LUCY: Oh, there's a lot more work. I wanted to call, / but—

TULLY: Doing any VCE subjects? Mum has me doing two.

LUCY: No.

TULLY: Why not?

LUCY: I don't know. The standard is a lot higher. And I don't want to be a doctor.

TULLY: You could be lawyer.

LUCY: Think I still wanna be a teacher.

TULLY: You're going to waste that scholarship on a teaching degree? Fuck off. You could have done that at Christ Our Saviour. At least I had dreams.

LUCY: I never wanted to do the exam. Dad made me.

TULLY: Mum wants you to tutor me in English / now—coz you're soo much smarter.

LUCY: Tully, you're the smartest person I know.

TULLY: Piss off. Apparently I'm not as stable or as hardworking as you are! 'Lucy won the Year Eight poetry competition—what did you ever do?'

LUCY: Tully … I mean, we could … meet for tutoring and just hang out if you want?

TULLY *walks away. Shift back to Laurinda.*

BRODIE: The A-team is holding rowing tryouts this morning for the C-team? As captain of the As, we'd like to see you there.

LUCY: I thought it was optional?

BRODIE: Hmm hah Lucy you are so adorable. Extracurricular activities are an integral part of the program that the school offers.

LUCY: Ah sorry I didn't / realise …

BRODIE: So while they are technically 'optional', activities like Saturday sport are actually essential. They form the well-rounded students who go on to be leaders. And as someone who gained entry on the EASY scholarship it's important that you find something else to help define you.

LUCY: I actually can't / do Saturdays. My mum—

BRODIE: I'm telling you this as your mentor. Think of me as your benefactor.

What are your ambitions Lucy? Hillary Clinton said in her speech at the World Conference in Beijing, 'My rights are human rights'. Do you understand?

LUCY: 'Women's rights are human rights.'

BRODIE: Because of this school you will have the chance to do anything. Excelling at extracurricular activities means future success. Rowers become Olympians. Debaters become attorney-generals.

LUCY: Yeah I know it's a good school, but Mum needs my help / on the weekends.

BRODIE: At Laurinda you have to make sacrifices. I am sure you, coming from where you do—

LUCY: Stanley?

BRODIE: Know what it is to make sacrifices.

LUCY: What do you mean? [*Morphing into* LUCY 37] What sacrifices have you made Brodie? Don't insult me or the people I grew up with. You have no idea what it is to sacrifice—

LINH *pops out of* BRODIE.

LINH: Hang on. You didn't say that. You barely said anything gutsy until *I* showed up! Stick to the rules or I'll have to turn this into a nightmare.

LUCY 37: I thought Brodie was being so nice trying to help me fit in. I just wanted her to like me.

LINH *rolls her eyes and resumes as* BRODIE.

BRODIE: You and Katie seem very close. She's so …

LUCY: She's been so generous … And so great at history … For the oral history presentation, she's got this amazing idea about how to present the Tsar Family and the mystery of Anastasia. It's like a murder mystery but from a modern day forensic scientist's perspective. She's like a walking encyclopedia—I'd be so lost without her.

BRODIE: I'm so glad you told me about your idea, because if you do the presentation that way, you're going to fail.

LUCY: But Katie said—

BRODIE: Look Lucy, Katie is, how do I say this … Katie is going to marry a lawyer, I'm going to be one. You need to decide which kind of woman you're going to be. This is your chance. Don't waste it.

AMBER *crashes into the room, followed by* CHELSEA *and* KATIE, *who are concerned for her welfare.*

AMBER *throws her bag down on the floor and wails.*

Gemma Chua-Tran in rehearsals for the Melbourne Theatre Company production of Laurinda. *Photo: Sarah Walker.*

KATIE: What's wrong, Amber?

AMBER: I'm so sorry Katie.

She begins to cry.

KATIE: Did you find out from your mum about the trick question? Have we all failed?

AMBER: I feel so guilty.

KATIE: Why? What happened?

CHELSEA: Oh my God! Did you lose the autograph?

KATIE: What? Not my Daniel Johns autograph! What happened to it?

AMBER: My dad's valuer lost it / I feel so bad.

KATIE: What?! No!!

CHELSEA: But you said / he'd get it valued!

AMBER: He thinks his wife put it out in the recycling.

CHELSEA: Oh no! Poor Katie.

KATIE: You promised me you would give it back. I chased Daniel Johns all over Chadstone. It was invaluable!

CHELSEA: To you.

KATIE: Yes! To me! I would die for Silverchair!

CHELSEA: [*patting* AMBER *on the back*] On the bright side, I suppose it must not have been worth as much as we thought.

KATIE: It was priceless to me Chelsea! Priceless. Daniel Johns!

KATIE *bursts into tears and leaves.*

The Cabinet all look at each other and gloat.

TRISHA *walks toward them—their next victim.*

BRODIE: [*sweetly*] Trisha!

CHELSEA: This'll be fun.

BRODIE: [*to* TRISHA] Trisha—look, we LOVE Beethoven and Tchaikovsky. But you've been playing a LOT. And we worry about your fingers.

TRISHA: Oh. They're fine. I do heaps of strength exercises. And guess what?! I just told Mrs Grey I'm finally ready to play the Ravel!

CHELSEA: So you've been organising all the performances yourself?

TRISHA: Yes.

CHELSEA: / Typical.

AMBER: No-one has been asking you to play?

TRISHA: No, to be the best you / need to practise.

CHELSEA: [*muttering*] I'd hate to be up myself.

TRISHA: Sorry Chelsea what did you say?

BRODIE: Don't you think the opportunities at Laurinda should be shared?

TRISHA: Do you want to play?

AMBER: [*quietly*] Trisha. Stop it. You're embarrassing yourself.

TRISHA: [*walking off*] Is Ravel embarrassing? Maybe I should play Stravinsky instead? Oh God, I was so sure about the Ravel, but now …

> LUCY *is silent and staring at the Cabinet—shocked by their behaviour.*

CHELSEA: What are you staring at?

AMBER: You would never do anything embarrassing would you Lucy?

LUCY: Oh um … no … The only thing I can play is 'Chopsticks'.

> *Beat. The Cabinet cackle.* AMBER *exits.*

BRODIE: That was so funny!

CHELSEA: Yeah Asians aren't usually funny! More like bad drivers.

> *The girls all laugh, then* LUCY, *reluctantly.*

> *The sound of coughing. At home.*

LUCY: *Mẹ có sao không?* (What's wrong?)

MUM: *Không có gì đâu. Mẹ ho tí thôi.* (Ah nothing. Just a cough.)

> MUM *coughs into a hanky. She feels breathless and takes a seat.*

LUCY: That's not nothing Mum. You're having trouble breathing.

MUM: *Mẹ không sao. Tại cái mớ vải này nè.* Bad batch. Don't tell dad. Go feed your brother, *ăn đi. Ểm ngồi trong cũi cả ngày rồi.* (I'm fine. It's the fabric. This is a bad batch. Don't tell your father. Go feed your brother. He's been in the play pen all day.)

LUCY: Okay Mum, but. *Con phải làm homework.* I don't have time to babysit. (Okay Mum, but then I've got homework.)

MUM: *Hồi xưa con đâu có phải làm nhiều homework như vậy đâu. I need you. Brother need you. Có nồi canh trên bếp á. Hâm lên đi.* (You never used to do this much homework. I need you. Your brother needs you. There's a pot of soup on the stove. Go warm it up.)

LUCY: Fine.

MUM: *Không được cãi!* (No backchat!)

LUCY: Yeah, well I can't every night now Mum, I'm doing remedial English, remember?

MUM: *Cái trường này dạy hỗn hả ta? School nó gửi letter về đó.* (That school is teaching you disrespect. They sent a letter.)

LUCY: You opened it?!

MUM: Your letter. My letter. *Thư nói gì vậy con?* (Your letter. My letter. What does it say?)

LUCY: Lucy is a delightful student and a pleasure to teach. She shouldn't be burdened with home duties.

MUM: *Xạo xạo không à. Nói thiệt coi,* what it say? (Cheeky girl. Now what does it say?)

LUCY: *Trường muốn con* … play sports on Saturdays. (The school just wants us to play sport on Saturdays.)

MUM: More school? More money? *Phí tiền, phí thời gian. Bộ chạy rượt theo banh là làm ra tiền hả.* Chase ball make you rich? (More school? More money? Waste of money and time. They think chasing after a ball will make them rich?)

> MUM *has a coughing fit.*

LUCY: *Mẹ đi doctor đi.* (Go to the doctor.)

MUM: *Chuyện ai nấy lo đi cô ơi. Nè, giúp mẹ việc nhà đi,* help sick mother—*ra chăm brother đi con.* (Mind your own business. Now do your duty and help your 'sick' mother—go look after your brother!)

> *In the classroom. Everyone is clapping except* KATIE *and* LUCY.

DR VANDERWERP: Brodie, Chelsea and Amber—what an inspired idea to set the murder of Anastasia in the science lab! A real forensic investigation. Now let me find your final history grade for this term. I know I had your other marks here somewhere …

> *The students groan.*

KATIE: [*whispering to the Cabinet*] Excuse me?! That was my idea.

BRODIE: Do you seriously think you could have pulled off something like that?

KATIE: Yes. Lucy and I had been planning the performance for weeks.

CHELSEA: Lamby? No way. No offence.

LUCY: You told me not to do it like that you knew we'd / been preparing.

BRODIE: Lucy, I've been meaning to thank you for the insider tip.

> BRODIE *winks.*

AMBER: To pull off a performance like that you need talent and an ability to hold an audience. Right?

CHELSEA: Yeah, we saved you the embarrassment.

KATIE: [*quietly to* LUCY] Why did you tell them?

LUCY: [*quietly to* KATIE] Brodie just, um, I never thought—

KATIE: It doesn't matter. They're right—our presentation wouldn't have been as good as theirs.

DR VANDERWERP: Ladies! [*Handing out their assessments*] I hope this is all the encouragement you need to pursue further study in history.

> DR VANDERWERP *sits on his desk. The girls look at their marks. The Cabinet are not happy.*

KATIE: Ha! Thank you, Dr V. I was so worried after our presentation!

DR VANDERWERP: It was excellent Katie. A little drier than I expected from you, but the content was exceptional.

CHELSEA: Just what you'd expect from a walking encyclopedia.

> LUCY *clocks the comment.* KATIE *looks over and sees* LUCY's *good mark—all is forgiven.*

> DR VANDERWERP *sits and takes a sip of his tea from his thermos.*

BRODIE: Dr Vanderwerp?

DR VANDERWERP: As I said before, I have assessed you on your work across the whole term.

AMBER: You never told us you were going to do that!

DR VANDERWERP: I believe you're mistaken Amber. I have been very clear.

BRODIE: The presentation we just did would have bumped up our term's marks to an A at least, wouldn't you say Dr Vanderwerp?

DR VANDERWERP: To be perfectly honest, all term, you three girls have been distracted—and, what's worse, distracting others. You don't seem to take history seriously.

BRODIE: Dr Vanderwerp—

DR VANDERWERP: If you would like to talk about this further, you can see me next period.

BRODIE: Next period?

DR VANDERWERP: Next period!

BRODIE: Next period. Yes. Sir.

    LUCY *comes home.* DAD *has three big bags of McDonald's.*

DAD: Where are your friends?

LUCY: What?

DAD: You usually bring your friends back. We are going to celebrate your good marks with food and a movie.

LUCY: I don't want anyone over! *Bạn con ai cũng busy hết, phải study mà Ba.* (They are all really busy studying Dad.)

DAD: Who's going to eat all this? *Chia sẻ văn hoá của mình với bạn cũng hay mà con.* Share our culture. (Who's going to eat all this? It would have been nice to share some of our culture with your friends.)

LUCY: McDonald's?

DAD: This is expensive food.

LUCY: *Bạn con không muốn đi all the way to Stanley để ăn Maccas and watch a film about the Vietnam War đâu ba ơi!* Like, seriously? (Dad, I really don't think the girls want to come all the way to Stanley to eat Maccas and watch a film about the Vietnam war. Like, seriously?)

DAD: It is serious! *Nó là lịch sử mà con, history! Con gái ba ashamed of culture của nước mình sao? Ba mẹ hi sinh chưa đủ sao—* (It is serious. Our history! I have a daughter who is so ashamed of her people? Did we not do enough—)

LUCY: Okay okay.

DAD: Okay okay? *Con phải biết hoà nhập ở trường mới. Chứ đừng giống Christ Our Saviour. You must make friends with rich people. Con phải thoát ra khỏi Stanley!* (Okay okay? You have to be sociable at your new school. You must make friends with rich people. You must get out of Stanley!)

    DAD *leaves.*

LUCY: [*under her breath*] What if I don't want to get out of Stanley?

    In the classroom.

CHELSEA: Quick! He's coming back. Shut the door.

    CHELSEA *runs to the desk, smears something on it and puts something in Dr Vanderwerp's thermos.*

LUCY and KATIE *enter.*

LUCY: Hey, what's happening?

BRODIE: Lucy, get in your seat now!

KATIE: But what are you doing?

CHELSEA: Bloody hell you two just sit down.

Stunned, KATIE *and* LUCY *find their seats.*

KATIE: Oh my God, what is that?

CHELSEA: Tampon and pigs' blood! Genius. This is gonna be so good.

LUCY: I really don't think—

CHELSEA: No-one cares what you think Lamby!

AMBER: The real genius is, it's parent teacher interviews for the Year Eleven and Twelves. The school is packed with parents!

LUCY *wants to say something.*

Everyone stares at their desk. Beat. Beat. Beat.

DR VANDERWERP *enters. Everything slows down.* DR VANDERWERP *takes his usual position perched on the corner of the desk, picks up his thermos and drinks it—stops—realises something is off—pulls the tampon out. Holds the bloody tampon out in front of him—shocked. There is a collective inhalation.* DR VANDERWERP *stands, confused. He sniffs and looks at his hand, it is covered in blood too. Blood?!*

DR VANDERWERP: [*sotto*] What the fuck?

Students stifle a giggle. DR VANDERWERP *looks at the students. Turns around to look at the desk and reveals his pants stained with blood.*

BRODIE: Oh, Dr Vanderwerp.

CHELSEA: Oh my God! Which one of you had your period all over the desk? That's not very hygienic.

[*Whispering*] Fucking brilliant. This prank will make history!

DR VANDERWERP *looks at his behind. Realises what has happened. The classroom disappears.*

LUCY: I should have stopped it!

KATIE: Stopped what?

LUCY: What they did to Dr V.

KATIE: The Cabinet play practical jokes all the time.

LUCY: What they did—

KATIE: I get that coming to a new school / and everything must—

LUCY: That wasn't a joke.

KATIE: It was funny.

LUCY: No-one was laughing.

KATIE: They will.

LUCY: Were you laughing when the Cabinet lost your Daniel Johns / autograph?

KATIE: Their valuer lost it. / I don't think—

LUCY: On purpose.

KATIE: No.

LUCY: Listen! I see the way things are and it's creepy—

KATIE: No. Lucy Lam. You see things as YOU are. And you see them wrong. The reason the school has a million-dollar library is because of Brodie's parents—Amber's parents donated money so we could take our school play to the Edinburgh Festival!

I get that you like don't get it coz, you're—from Stanley … a Catholic … Asian and all that.

LINH appears as if from LUCY's *body. This is the moment in* LUCY's *memory where she psychologically splits. She has her outside self* (LUCY) *and her inner thoughts* (LINH). LUCY *screams in pain and clutches her heart—she is in pain the whole scene.*

LUCY: Argh!

LINH: Are you going to take this shit.

KATIE: Oh my God are you okay?

LUCY 37: I'd forgotten how much your arrival hurt!

LINH: Yup—banana split.

LUCY *rubs her chest.*

KATIE: Lucy? Are you alright?? Do you have a heart condition?

LUCY: Sorry, Katie. I'm just … [*To* LINH] Why now?

LINH: Because you bend and bend and bend and then you break. Say something … you can do it.

LUCY 37: To Katie? But she's nice.

KATIE: Thank / you?

LINH: She's a Cabinet sympathiser.

LUCY 37: It's more complicated than / that.

KATIE: Is it?

LUCY 37: [*in pain, rubbing her chest*] Fuck!

KATIE: You just said the f-word!

LINH: Oh, yeah, not Asian and respectful / enough?

LUCY 37: Shut up!

KATIE: Lucy! I'm only trying to help you! The Cabinet do what they do and there's nothing we can do about it. If I learnt anything from my mum is that they can destroy your life. It's better just to let them do their thing. Lucy. Please. Listen to me. My mum NEVER recovered—I'm going to survive this—Don't do anything to jeopardise your place here. For my sake—I like having a friend.

LUCY 37: I don't remember it happening like this.

LINH: This is exactly how it happened.

KATIE: What's happening?

> LINH *grabs* LUCY*'s hand.*

LUCY / LINH: Katie! Shut up. These girls are bitches! They treat everyone like shit. You know and you keep taking it. Are you going to be a punching bag the rest of your life? I'm not.

LINH: Doesn't it feel better to get that off your chest!

KATIE: That's the whole point Lucy. I'm making sure they—this won't define me. I want life to be more than high school!

> KATIE *walks off.*

LUCY: Oh—I've got to apologise!

LINH: Ah ah ah. No you don't …

> LINH *clicks her fingers and* MUM *storms in.*

MUM: *Sao con không qua giúp Toolly làm homework. Mẹ xấu hổ thiệt luôn á. You say yes and you don't do. Con nghĩ giờ con học private school là con ngon lắm rồi phải không?* (Why are you not helping Toolly with her school homework. I am ashamed. Why would you say yes and not do it? You think you're above us now that you go to private school?)

LUCY: Tully didn't want my help.

MUM: *Mẹ không hiểu cái rich school đó đang dạy con cái gì nữa.* (I don't know what that rich school is teaching you.)

LINH: What IS that school teaching you Lucy?

LUCY: She doesn't want to see me.

MUM: *Con đã quên mình là ai rồi!* (You're forgetting yourself!)

LUCY: No Mum, they've forgotten me and you don't even like Tully.

MUM: *Gia đình là trên hết! Family first! Toolly mother là chúa gossip cái vùng này biết không. Bả lúc nào cũng gossip lúc bán thịt. 'Bà biết Toolly nhà tui không? Toolly nhà tui sẽ làm doctor.' Con muốn mẹ mất mặt hả? Mình phải dựa vào cái community này mà sống. Nhớ chưa?* (Family first! And her mother is the gossip queen of this town. Always talking while selling meat. 'Did you hear about my Toolly? Did you know that my Toolllly will be a doctor? Do you want me to lose face? This community is all we have. Don't forget that.)

LINH: Oh Mum's not happy.

LUCY 37: [*to* LINH] Okay enough! [*To* MUM, *as* LUCY] You don't understand anything. You've never understood.

MUM: *Con nhỏ này sướng mà vẫn cứ kêu can.* I understand everything. (Ungrateful child. I understand everything.)

> MUM *exits.*

LINH: Haven't you missed me? You keep squashing me down. But now I'm freeeeeeee!

> *The freedom ballet.*

> *The library.* LUCY*'s eye is twitching again.*

I really like hanging out. You so need me. You don't need those rich bitches—sheltered and shut off but brimming with stifled sex. That's why they're so mean.

> LINH *mocks* BRODIE.

'My rights are human rights. I have the right. I'm always right.'

> LINH *and* LUCY *laugh in spite of themselves.*

Quick, Katie's at three o'clock.

> LINH *grabs* LUCY*'s hands to wave at* KATIE, *while she is picking up a book.* LUCY *resists and they have a tussle over it. She ends up throwing the book across the room.*

KATIE: Hey! I tried calling you but I couldn't get through and I was thinking about what you said and what I said. And I think it had been a day—like you know with the blood and everything and maybe we just were you know, like on different like wavelengths? It's just … It's better to just like let the Cabinet like do their thing—they can really make it hard otherwise—

LUCY: Yeah you told me. I've got a lot of work to finish for Mrs Leslie. It's really hard for me with English as a second language.

LINH: Phoar. That's brutal—

KATIE: Oh okay … It's just that everyone is talking about Dr Vanderwerp. Chelsea said he couldn't hack it and that's why he's like gone. Amber said he like deserved what he got coz he was unfit to teach. But I found out from like listening in on a staff meeting that he's out on stress leave! Do you think that like that prank sent him over the edge? It would be awful / if you were like right.

LUCY: Remedial remember? I have to think about my future.

KATIE: Oh. Okay. Well. I'll be having lunch on the oval and revising trig if you like wanna join.

> KATIE *leaves.* AMBER *and* CHELSEA *walk past. They wave at* LUCY. LINH *controls* LUCY*'s hand so that she can't wave and instead hits herself in the head. The Cabinet look at* LUCY *and she tries to smile as her hand is pressed to her head.*

LINH: Why are you hitting yourself? Why are you hitting yourself? Stop twitching. Stop twitching. Ha.

> LUCY *doesn't laugh and scowls at* LINH.

Come on! Talk to me.

LUCY 37: You're as annoying now as you were then. You sent me back in time. Fine. I'm here. I'll relive it and get it right this time. Isn't that the point? You know, I was doing fine until you showed up.

LINH: No, you weren't. And getting it right isn't the point.

> You need to see—Oh no. Leslie's coming back. Wish I could delete her. So racist.

> MRS LESLIE *walks into library.*

LUCY 37: She wasn't racist, was she? I liked Mrs Leslie! She's was so nice and she's the only one who made me feel smart … Hi, Mrs Leslie. I'm just finishing off the *Gatsby* task.

MRS LESLIE: Oh I am impressed. If only all the girls worked as hard as you do.

Now *Gatsby*, are you ready? Remember, no generalisations or stereotypes. If you want to return to regular English we need specifics. The green light what does it mean?

CHARLOTTE: I don't understand anything in this book, Miss.

LUCY 37: What's Charlotte doing here?

LINH: Can't you see the connection?

MRS LESLIE: Lucy?

CHARLOTTE: These books are bullshit—they don't mean anything to us.

LUCY 37: Well, the green light is supposed to be a metaphor for Gatsby's hope, because it is far away and flashes and blinks, to emphasise that hope is often elusive.

CHARLOTTE: Who cares?

LUCY 37: But no-one ever speaks about Gatsby's envy, which the green could also symbolise.

CHARLOTTE: Why do we have to study this shit?

MRS LESLIE: You're really getting the hang of this Lucy.

LUCY 37: Who would Gatsby be, if he lived in our area?

CHARLOTTE: I don't care about a rich gay guy in a pink suit.

MRS LESLIE: That's the type of question we expect of our students.

LUCY 37: What do you mean?

MRS LESLIE: You will be with your classmates sooner than you think.

CHARLOTTE: I dunno, he's just tryna look better than he is—like everyone here just gagging for the big rich houses over the tracks.

LUCY 37: Yes!

MRS LESLIE: I'll miss our sessions.

CHARLOTTE: Why aren't we reading about the history of THIS land and the First People? Or I dunno, likes … If it's gonna be something like *Gatsby* can we read about rich gay Asians?

LUCY 37: I agree with you but sometimes by suspending our disbelief with a story that feels very far away—we understand our own story better.

CHARLOTTE: You're a good teacher Miss, but you've sold out.

CHARLOTTE *disappears.*

MRS LESLIE: Wise beyond your years! I knew it, as soon as I read your story about being a young child standing next to your grandmother in Cho Lon, helping to sell boiled eggs. Oh, it was just too beautiful. It was just so simple … so … special.

LINH: Would she think that if it was set in Stanley?

Beat.

LUCY: Mrs Leslie, I wanted to talk to you about something.

MRS LESLIE: What is it dear?

LUCY: There have just been some things going on.

LINH: Remember what Katie said—

MRS GREY *appears—we're in two spaces at once again.*

MRS LESLIE: Oh? What sort of things, Lucy?

LUCY: Well, I, um … I wanted to talk about Dr Vanderwerp.

MRS LESLIE: What do you mean dear?

LINH: They screwed him over massively.

MRS GREY: Lucy, I don't know how informal your previous student teacher relationships were, but you have been overly familiar with Mrs Leslie. Additionally, you are not integrating in the way we had hoped.

LUCY: I think we caused Dr Vanderwerp to quit.

MRS LESLIE: How do you mean you caused him to quit?

LUCY: Well, what happened in class …

MRS LESLIE: Oh, Lucy! Dr Vanderwerp has just taken a term off. Family-related matters. Have you been worried about him?

MRS GREY: Your results have been adequate, but not exceptional … and you blatantly refuse to participate in extracurricular activities …

MRS LESLIE: You sweet thing.

LUCY: But the last day of Term One—

MRS LESLIE: Oh Dr Vanderwerp wasn't rattled by a silly prank Lucy.

MRS GREY: Need I remind you, you are on a scholarship? Your conduct across all things must be exemplary.

MRS LESLIE: When I was a student here we pranked our teachers all the time!

We had a Home Ec teacher—mean as anything—one day we all hid our oven timers in the fan vents where she couldn't reach. We timed them to go off every two minutes.

Thirty girls, thirty timers! Ringing every two minutes! The

noise! Ha. Can you imagine?

She laughs.

Growing up sometimes means testing your boundaries. My daughter Amber could learn a lot from you. I dare say even open her eyes to her self-centered ways.

MRS GREY: We offer you the best, and we expect the best. The other Asians are excelling in this environment. Why aren't you?

LINH: Why aren't you as good as the other Asians?

LUCY: I like Amber.

MRS LESLIE: Well, why don't you come over tomorrow night for a study date?

MRS GREY: Mrs Leslie believes you are ready for the classroom. These next steps will define you, Lucy. Don't sink. Lean into your peer mentors. They will help you swim. Are you ready?

LUCY: Yes. I am ready to do what it takes.

MRS GREY *disappears.*

LINH: Kill me.

LUCY: [*to* LINH] Maybe Tully was right. Maybe I want to be a doctor.

MRS LESLIE: Well I don't know a Tully, but bully for you.

LUCY's *eye starts twitching.*

MRS LESLIE's *home descends.* LUCY *sits awkwardly and* LINH *hands her a cup of tea.*

LINH: What is it with manicured lawns and Roman columns?

LUCY 37: We're at Leslie's house.

LINH: Dad would lose his shit! Look at the size of that wall! 'The concrete rendering is very beautiful. My nephew is a renderer on the Gold coast.'

[*Imitating Mrs Leslie*] 'Darling, that's sandstone imported from NSW at the turn of the century.'

She dances around the house.

Wonder what Mr Leslie does?

LUCY: Will you shut up! Mrs Leslie has been so nice to me. And you heard Grey, I just need to fit in better—you're not making it / easy.

LINH: Fit in? With these cows?

LUCY: If I get in with the Cabinet it'll solve everything. I'll get Mrs Grey off my back, / I'll get to—

LINH: YOU WANT TO GET IN THE CABINET?!

> LINH *is on the floor, laughing.*

Oh my God, you think you'll get into the cabinet … hey here's a cabinet.

> *She mimes a cabinet door and opens it.*

Full of oven timers timed to go off every two minutes! Little bombs everywhere … Can you believe what the Cabinet mums did to Katie's mum? This shit is learned behavior. Can see why you want in.

> LINH *spots the notebook and throws it toward* LUCY.

Ha—Look at this! Amber had the Silverchair notebook all along!

LUCY: Oh my God!

LINH: [*throwing the notebook to* LUCY] They make me wanna spew. Catch!

MRS LESLIE: [*offstage*] What was that dear?

LUCY: Oh my God!

> LUCY *closes the notebook and puts it in her lap as* MRS LESLIE *walks in.*

I've never seen a didgeridoo like that before.

MRS LESLIE: [*entering*] Oh, Lucy, it's a Yidaki played by the Indigenous peoples of Arnhem land. I picked it up from a little art gallery there on our recent trip. It's authentic. I have the certificate which says so.

> *She laughs.*

How's your Oolong tea? I have a wonderful collection of teas from all around the world. I love Oolong. It's good for my metabolism. But I'm sure you already knew that.

LUCY: Where's Amber?

MRS LESLIE: She'll be along momentarily from orchestra rehearsal. Lucy, I have to be honest, my intentions here aren't completely pure … I want the two of you to be friends. You don't seem to have any and she could learn a lot from you.

LINH: Rude. We don't need Amber's friendship, kay?

MRS LESLIE: I worry about her.

LINH: You don't need the Cabinet to survive Laurinda.

MRS LESLIE: You are such a wise, hard-working, self-contained little hive of industry.

LINH: Tell her about Tully's cousin Ming with his prison time. See how warm she is then!

AMBER *walks in.*

AMBER: What's she doing here? She's not like Zi Wei or June Moon, Mum. They went back to Asia, back to their rich mums and dads. You collect Asians like your teas.

LINH *and* LUCY *spray Oolong tea everywhere. A moment between* AMBER *and* LUCY.

MRS LESLIE: That's enough, young lady.

AMBER *ignores her mother and spies the notebook on* LUCY's *lap.*

LUCY: [*referring to the notebook*] Yeah, I saw this on the bench.

AMBER: Yeah and?

LINH: What you gotta say to that?

LUCY: I just thought—it's nothing.

LINH: What?

LUCY *smiles.*

MRS LESLIE: Lucy, I would like your advice for Amber's party. We can't agree on the decor.

AMBER *grabs the catalogue.*

So, Lucy you'll come of course, won't you?

LINH: Haha look at Amber's face.

LUCY: If Amber would like me there.

MRS LESLIE: Good. I've ordered this palette scheme.

LINH: You don't seriously want to go, do you?

LUCY: It looks vibrant! Would you like me to bring anything?

AMBER: Mum it's *my* birthday

MRS LESLIE: Enough Amber. [*To* LUCY] It's all catered for.

AMBER: [*storming out*] You are such a control freak! I never get to do anything!

MRS LESLIE: [*hissing / calling out after her*] I've just about had enough of you, young lady! [*To* LUCY] I don't want your mother to go to any trouble.

> LINH *snaps her fingers. 'Champagne Supernova' cuts in.* AMBER*'s party. Animal themed.* LUCY *has cat ears on and is holding a tray of rice paper rolls. There are no young people around. People at the party think that she is a waitress.*

LINH: Amber's party—woooohooo! Can you put that tray down?
That's right! Soo many old white people at a young person's party—looks like a theatre foyer.

LUCY 37: Why are we here? I don't want to be here. This isn't an unpleasant memory? It was just a stupid party. Oh, what was I wearing?

LINH: I don't know why you've got such an issue with it, you look great. Remember, Amber had this mountain of presents.

LUCY 37: Yeah, I convinced Mum to make Amber's skirt. She spent all afternoon on it. She made me feel so guilty.

LINH: Jungle theme.

LUCY 37: So many presents.

LINH: Yeah you were dressed all wrong.

> MRS LESLIE *grabs a rice paper roll.*

MRS LESLIE: Lucy! I didn't recognise you! What are you doing serving the guests? Why aren't you partying in the other room with your friends! Getting … jiggy with it.

> *She takes a bite of the rice paper roll and has a little orgasmic moment that goes too long.*

LUCY: Oh I—

MRS LESLIE: These rice paper rolls are delicious. Your mother made these?!

LUCY: Yup. She'll be so glad to hear it. They have a Teochew influence because she's used to cooking for Dad.

MRS LESLIE: Is that a Vietnamese spice?

LUCY: No, Mum is Vietnamese, but Dad is Teochew.

LINH: [*waving at a guest*] I. am. Asia! .

LUCY: Shhhhh.

MRS LESLIE: I'll keep it quiet. Promise!

LUCY: His ancestry is from Guangdong, in the south of China.

> MRS LESLIE *is not convinced.*

MRS LESLIE: Do you speak Too-choo at home?

LUCY: Mainly Vietnamese. Dad would make Mum speak English if she wasn't so bad at it.
It's nice to be able to talk to someone about this stuff.

MRS LESLIE: I would love a cooking lesson. Would your mother be interested?

LINH: [*laughing*] Ha! [*Imitating Mum*] *Gì? Mấy bả muốn mẹ bỏ work show them how to cook something?* (What? They want me to leave my work and show them how to cook something?)

MRS LESLIE: Of course I would pay for her time and ingredients. How much money would you need? Five hundred dollars? Would that …

> LINH *snaps her fingers. The party shifts / spins.*

DR VANDERWERP: Oh Lucy! Well, this is unexpected. I was hoping to slip out without being noticed.

LUCY 37: Dr Vanderwerp! What are you doing here? I don't remember you being at the party. Are you okay? You look …

DR VANDERWERP: [*referring to the rice paper rolls*] They are paying you aren't they?

LUCY: What?

LINH: Goddamn it Lucy. Put the tray down. Down down!

> *Guest walks by, grabbing a rice paper roll. Another puts the serviette in* LUCY's *hand.* DR VANDERWERP *is distracted by the music.*

LUCY: Oh. No. I'm just … Dr V … I wanted to say—I, I feel … I should have—

> *Flash. Someone has taken a photo of Dr Vanderwerp and Lucy. It's* CHELSEA *and* AMBER, *cackling in coordinated outfits.*

LINH: Here they are. And I'm out—gotta change. Brodie looked amaze!

CHELSEA: Yum. You seriously need to get a life Dr V. I am not going out with you!

DR VANDERWERP: Very funny Chel—

AMBER: He's just here for my mum's wallet.

'Fastlove' by George Michael plays as they enter the actual party. DR VANDERWERP *leaves.*

Come and dance the next one with us, Lucy! Don't spend my party chatting up grovelling teachers!

LUCY: / I wasn't …

AMBER: Hey, thank you! I just opened my presents. I can't believe you got me that skirt. I didn't even know they were in Sportsgirl yet.

LUCY: They aren't. My mum … / has connections.

AMBER: Oh my God! I didn't know she worked in retail! My aunt does too! She's an executive at Myer.

CHELSEA: You should have seen the look on Amber's mum's face.

AMBER: I love it. Don't worry she didn't realise it was from you.

CHELSEA: You're a dark horse.

AMBER: Maybe I misjudged you.

CHELSEA: Maybe Brodie was right. Maybe you're not like Katie, that dibbing dobbing bitch. We know your former friend dobbed on us Lucy to Mrs Grey.

LUCY: Dobbed on you?

CHELSEA: About Dr V. There's no need to protect Katie.

AMBER: Yeah! She did it because she wasn't invited to the party.

LUCY: I didn't know that.

AMBER: The look on her face!

The girls laugh and LUCY *joins in half-heartedly. Another song comes on.*

CHELSEA: This is the wrong song. DJ! Come on, give us something.

Medley of nineties music.

Errrrrmerrrrrgerrrrd Yes!! I love this song.

BRODIE *appears—she looks incredible! She sings: 'No matter how hard I try, you keep pushing me aside and I can't break through, there's no talking to you …'*

LUCY 37: This definitely wasn't playing.

LINH: Bit of poetic license.

On the dance floor CHELSEA *joins* BRODIE, *and the Cabinet begin dancing. A crowd gathers. They have clearly practised this.*

LUCY *cannot dance but attempts the moves. The Cabinet finish their dance and* LUCY *keeps going.*

LUCY 37: I can't believe you're making me do this again! Make my body stop!

While LUCY*'s dancing is phenomenally bad it is mesmerising to the point of being formally interesting.*

AMBER: I had no idea you had that in you.

BRODIE: You're going to help us make history, Lucy Lam.

CHELSEA: What do you mean?

BRODIE: I thought it was obvious! We're making Lucy part of the Cabinet.

The Cabinet all start clapping and laughing, AMBER *and* CHELSEA *half-heartedly.* LUCY *keeps dancing, and joins in the clap, despite herself.*

LINH *clicks. Another memory. Music shifts—Kenny G. Back with the Cabinet mums.* MRS WHITE *has been drinking.* LUCY *is holding the food tray.*

MRS WHITE: [*grabbing a rice paper roll*] Diane! I want the caterer's number! Those spring rolls are to die for!

MRS LESLIE: Lucy's mother made them! I'm trying to convince Lucy to get her mother to share her culinary expertise with us.

MRS NEWBERRY: So, this is your *Pygmalion* project!

LUCY 37: Project?

MRS LESLIE: Oh Lucy, how rude of me, this is Gloria and Margaret. You know their daughters, Brodie and Chelsea.

MRS NEWBERRY *extends her hand to* LUCY, *who shakes it, as:*

MRS NEWBERRY: [*singing*] 'Lots of chocolate for me to eat. Lots of coal makin' lots of heat.'

MRS WHITE *joins in with the song.*

MRS NEWBERRY / MRS WHITE: 'Warm face, warm hands. / Warm feet. Oh wouldn't—'

MRS LESLIE: Katie Gladrock clamoured to be Lucy's mentor at the start of the year.

MRS NEWBERRY: Gracie Gladrock's daughter?

MRS LESLIE: Yes. Dull child.

MRS WHITE: [*laughing*] To think if you'd spread your legs like Gracie, things would have been very different.

MRS LESLIE: Oh dear. I'm sure Lucy doesn't want to hear this.

MRS WHITE: I'm sure someone from *Stanley* has heard far worse!

MRS NEWBERRY: [*grabbing Lucy's arm*] The. Things. You. Must. Have. Gone. Through.

MRS LESLIE: You must never mention this to Katie.

MRS WHITE: Every time I look at Katie, I think of Gracie and Home Ec and can't stop laughing.

LUCY: You mean when you hid the oven timers?

MRS WHITE: No no no no. The oven timers were a sweet enhancement Diane thought up because she didn't want to go through with our plan.

MRS LESLIE: Lucy doesn't need to hear about our antics.

MRS WHITE: [*laughing*] She's still funny about it! If we hadn't greased the floor with Vaseline, we would have had to keep enduring her classes.

MRS NEWBERRY: And you did put the empty Vaseline containers in Gracie's locker.

MRS LESLIE: Well … under duress.

MRS WHITE: We did some cleaning up. Best years of my life.

MRS NEWBERRY: Best looking ones too.

> *The mothers cackle.*

MRS WHITE: They were even both at hospital at the same time—the old bat recovering from her hip surgery and Gracie, [*whispering*] to have the baby …

MRS LESLIE: Gloria! I think you've had enough. / [*To* LUCY] Thank God Katie has her grandmother.

MRS WHITE: What?

MRS NEWBERRY: Reputation matters.

> LINH *clicks—Things whirlwind—the party is over.*

> *At home.*

LUCY 37: Will you stop moving through these memories so quickly / I feel sick.

MUM: *Ủa? Sao con không mang mấy cái tray về?* (What do you mean you left my trays?)

LUCY: *Mọi người còn dùng mà.* (They were still using them)

MUM: *Con nhớ là phải lấy tray về đó.* Three dollar each. (You'd better make sure that they come back. They cost me three dollars each.)

LUCY: Okay. Okay Mum. I'll get your trays back. / I'm going to bed.

MUM: Okay okay Mum? *Mẹ là bạn ngang hàng của con hả? Best friend? Con về sớm thì ra đây phụ mẹ cho xong lô này coi.* (Okay okay Mum?! Am I your best friend now? Since you're home early you can help me finish this batch.)

LUCY: Mum, I am too tired. I'll help you in the morning.

MUM: *Hay quá. Mẹ vừa làm two hundred rolls, mẹ cuốn cuốn cuốn cho bạn của con, vậy mà con tirrrred. Dad đang làm tăng ca, extra shift kìa. Ngồi xuống.* (I just hand rolled two hundred rice paper rolls for your friends and you are tired. Your dad is doing an extra shift. Sit.)

> LUCY *reluctantly sits down and begins helping her mum fix buttonholes. They sit in silence sewing shirt pockets.*
>
> LUCY*'s eye begins twitching—it's distracting her—she accidently tears the buttonhole she was making.*

LUCY: Shit.

MUM: *Con làm cái gì vậy? Con có biết mẹ làm bao lâu mới xong cái này không?* (What have you done? Do you know how long it took me to make this?)

LUCY: Sorry.

MUM: Sorry sorry?? Will sorry pay for this? *Nguyên một buổi chiều mẹ may skirt cho sinh nhật rich friend của con. Không nghe được một lời thank you. Như vậy là mẹ bị trừ tiền lương rồi.* (Sorry? Sorry? Will sorry pay for this? Spent all afternoon making a skirt for your rich friend's birthday? Not even a thank you. This is coming out of my pay!)

LUCY: Out of your pay? What?! That isn't fair.

MUM: Nothing in life fair. *Mấy cái áo này phải giao tomorrow, sáng sớm. Mẹ không kịp may nguyên một cái shirt mới đâu. Con có thể coi thường việc này, nhưng mấy cái áo này mua cơm cho con ăn mỗi tối đó.* This your bowl of rice. (Nothing in life is fair. These shirts are being picked up tomorrow—early. I can't make an entire shirt before then. You might not think this is important, but this shirt buys your bowl of rice every night.)

MUM *exits.*

LUCY: I'm sorry okay?

LUCY *crumples.* LINH *comes out of nowhere.*

Urghgh. Go away!

LINH: Mission accomplished you're in the Cabinet! [*Passing an imaginary microphone*] How does it feel?

LUCY: You know what Linh? It feels good. It feels fucking fantastic.

LINH: What?

LUCY: Yeah—I feel good when I'm around them.

LINH: You'll never be equal.

LUCY: The closer I am, the less likely they are to eat me.

LINH: You're such a cliché.

LUCY: They make me feel part of something.

LINH: Yup. I can see it. You fit right in. Those dance moves were something else.

LUCY: I want stuff now. Like I never wanted before. I never used to wake at night wanting things. Everything here is cheap and tacky. All the trees look like shrubs—everything is fake—fake Louis Vitton, Chanel bags—it's all junk. This house is full of crap. None of those girls live in piles of cheap crap. None of them have to help their parents sew shirts. None of them have to look after their siblings.

Everyone at Christ Our Savior lives in the same dumpy houses, so I never realised. I was too busy helping Mum make summer shorts with fabric scraps.

LINH: You were happy.

LUCY: Well, now I want more. And I have to stand out in the right way. I can't debate Linh, I don't have an instrument, my only sport is soccer—

LINH: The only reason you're in the Cabinet is because you make them look better. Can you even hear yourself? Do you think Tully would have done the same. She wouldn't.—

LUCY: She would! I'm working as hard as ever, but they're playing a game and I don't know the rules.

LINH: Play your own game.

LUCY: But I want to play theirs.

LINH: You don't know their rules.

LUCY: I'm gonna learn them!

LINH: But they can't explain them.

LUCY: Why not?

LINH: Because they were born into them.

LUCY: Well I'm going to try. I don't want to be *this* anymore!

LINH: Well … if THIS isn't what you want.

You don't need me. I'm out.

LINH disappears. Everything is suddenly very quiet.

LUCY 37: We were so dramatic! I couldn't believe that you left! Linh? You there?

Silence.

Linh? This isn't funny. You can't leave me now—and then—at the same time! What am I meant to do?!

She clicks her fingers.

Linh!! This is very unresolved. Very irresponsible. You just don't ditch someone mid—mid—whatever this is!

Hello? Hello! You can't leave me all alone—again!

Beat.

They were helpful and accommodating and accepting! It was a small sacrifice. It's what everyone wanted, Mrs Grey, my dad? That was how I was going to get out of Stanley. It was nineteen ninety-seven—I couldn't see how else I was going to get through.

The eye twitch is back. LUCY *clicks again.*

Image of LUCY *with the Cabinet. They all work together. Giggle. Look at* LUCY. LUCY *feels unsettled.*

The world spins. MRS GREY *appears.*

MRS GREY: Lucy, you will be providing the colloquy on behalf of the school at the Equity in Education conference at Melbourne University. Meredith Grammar is sending three of its Indigenous access students along to do a dance. Brodie has volunteered to help you. Your former principal informed us that you were passionately involved in school activities. This will be good for you Lucy. An opportunity. To become a Laurindan leader.

LUCY *clicks.*

BRODIE *sidles up to* LUCY.

LUCY 37: Okay Linh, enough.

BRODIE: Look, I love what you've done—

LUCY 37: Linh?

BRODIE: —with the Equity in Education speech but I was thinking—

LUCY 37: So, what, you're not going to talk to me at all?

BRODIE: —that you could talk about the difference between Laurinda and your old / school's academic standards.

LUCY 37: —school's academic standards.

> LUCY *is resigned to the fact that* LINH *isn't going to talk to her.*

Okay fine. How did you get my speech?

BRODIE: I'm trying to help you Lucy. It's important that you represent the school—and yourself—well.

LUCY: Thanks Brodie. I've got my conference talk under control. I was in the SRC at my old school and had to present all the time.

BRODIE: Lucy. That's so sweet but you're not in Stanley anymore.

LUCY: I'll just talk about how povvo my old school was and how it's a hundred times better here.

BRODIE: I can see where you're going with that but I think I can help navigate the nuance of that argument better.

> *Beat.*

LUCY: Really Brodie, I appreciate all the help. And support. And guidance. And the way you have made me feel so included.

> *Her eye twitches.*

You've tried to be inclusive. Thank you. But I think this time I'm fine.

BRODIE: There's a way to express yourself at these things, so people will listen and respect you.

LUCY: Respect? Of course, you're such an expert on respect. Laurinda has such a culture of fairness and respect towards its students and teachers.

> *Beat.*

BRODIE: [*sickly sweet*] Lucy … look … if you don't want this, there would be no shame in renouncing your scholarship and providing someone else who really wants it with the opportunity. Maybe all this isn't right for you? Maybe you're not ready. And that's okay. We would hate to throw you overboard and send you back where you came from. It should be your choice if you don't want to be here.

LUCY *goes to leave.*

Where are you going?

LUCY: Where am I going? Back to where I came from.

Do I have your permission to go to the toilet?

BRODIE: No, you caaaaaaaaaan't!

LUCY: Brodie, there's no need to be rude!

LUCY *walks away and heads to the toilets.* TRISHA *is there waiting for the loo.* LUCY *checks the cubicles—there is one on the end that is occupied.*

They are disgusting! I thought the girls here were meant to be examples to the rest of us!

TRISHA: Yeah, they stink so bad. I've come in twice in the last half hour but the last one is never free.

LUCY: I really enjoy your playing in assembly. I really mean that.

TRISHA: I don't do it for the applause but it's nice when I get it.

TRISHA *leaves.* LUCY *hangs around waiting for the last cubicle.* BRODIE *walks in.* LUCY *opens her mouth to speak,* BRODIE *shushes her with a finger to the lips.* AMBER *and* CHELSEA *walk in. They exchange a look.* AMBER *nods.* CHELSEA *readies herself in front of the closed toilet. Then swings her body around and kicks open the door. A sound like a snapped chicken wing. And then a howl.*

KATIE: Ahhhh. Eeeee. Oohhhhh.

She whimpers.

The cubicle door now swings open to reveal KATIE *with underpants around her knees, clutching her left hand with her right.*

LUCY: Katie?!

BRODIE: Oh my God! Oh my God!

CHELSEA: What—

KATIE: Oh my hand. My hand. It's broken.

LUCY: / Are you okay?

BRODIE: Oh, oh, oh. Why are *you* in there? Oh no, oh no. Get up.

KATIE *stands.*

This wasn't meant to happen. Damn it Amber! This is your fault. I thought you said Trisha was still in there.

TRISHA *walks in.*

AMBER: But I saw her go in! I saw her walk into the toilet block! [*To* TRISHA] I saw you walk in!

TRISHA: Yeah I just walked in because I've been needing to go for ages, and I still need to gooooo. Urghghg but the last cubicle is like never free … and the other two are covered in … poo … Katie. You okay?

LUCY: Is your hand really broken?

KATIE: I think so.

TRISHA: How did you break your hand?

KATIE: Wooh I feel dizzy.

Woozy, KATIE *lies down on the toilet floor.*

CHELSEA: Why didn't you bloody tell us it wasn't her?

KATIE: [*to* TRISHA] I put my hand on the lock because I thought someone was going to jimmy the door. If I had my hands on my knees this wouldn't have happened. I'm sure it was an accident.

BRODIE: Of course it / was

LUCY: No / it wasn't.

BRODIE: Katie, are you okay? You don't look / good.

LUCY: Why would you do that?

BRODIE: [*to* LUCY] We did not want to get you involved in this.

TRISHA: Did you think I was in the toilet?

KATIE: Um … I'm not feeling so well.

AMBER: We should have told her.

CHELSEA: She's not really part of us. We are the Cabinet. *She* started the whole thing, anyway.

LUCY: Oh yeah? How did I start it? By clapping loudly?

CHELSEA: You created a megalomaniac who thinks she's top shit.

TRISHA: Did you want to break my hand?

LUCY: People like her music at assembly! Where is the crime in that?

TRISHA: You think I'm a megalomaniac?

LUCY: What is wrong with you three?

BRODIE: Let's go to the school nurse.

BRODIE *and* KATIE *leave.*

TRISHA: But then I couldn't play.

>*Beat.*

If no-one is using it. I really need to go.

>TRISHA *enters the cubicle.*

AMBER: I don't get why you're everyone's favourite. If I pulled the kind of shit you do—

LUCY: Favourite?

AMBER: Everyone's always talking about you. 'What subjects do you think Lucy should do? What if we got her to speak at the parents' fundraiser?' You're everyone's special project. I wish I was Asian. They get everything!

>LUCY *clicks.*

LUCY: What are you doing in my house?

BRODIE: I didn't know you had a brother! He's such a cute baby.

>You live a really long way away. I caught a cab.

LUCY 37: [*to* LINH, *who isn't there*] Linh, I don't want to do this anymore!

BRODIE: Lucy. I'm worried about you. Is it the conference? Because, as a woman I understand how you feel. It's tough to find a voice in a world set against you. But everyone can succeed if they work hard enough.

LUCY: Were you working hard when you broke Katie's hand?

BRODIE: She's fine. Accidents happen. No-one is concerned. It's only a hairline fracture.

LUCY: But we both know the truth, Brodie.

BRODIE: From day one we've taken you under our wing. We care about what happens to you. That's why I put you forward for the Equity in Education Conference.

LUCY: You, what?

BRODIE: You're being very hostile. Do you want me to go because of the shady deal your mum was doing as I arrived. Why did she have all that cash?

LUCY: Oh piss off.

BRODIE: Oh you make things impossible! I didn't want to tell you this—but—you are at Laurinda, because my mum and dad funded the scholarship. They know it is so important to lift people out of poverty. Do you want to live here the rest of your life?

BRODIE *leaves.* LUCY *crumples.*

MUM: *Con sao vậy? Con bị bệnh hả?* (What's wrong? Are you sick?)

LUCY *doesn't respond.*

Ra giúp mẹ làm lô mới được không. Help. Rồi mẹ sẽ call school nói là con không đi học được. (Come and help me with the next batch. We can call the school and tell them you can't go.)

LUCY *composes herself. She sits with* MUM, *picks up a shirt and scissors and cleans the shirt stitches. Silence.*

MUM *starts singing a lullaby.*

LUCY: You haven't sung this since I was little.

MUM*'s singing is interrupted by a cough.*

Me? (Mum?)

MUM *waves her off. They sit in silence for a moment.*

MUM: *Hôm bữa bạn con qua đây làm gì dợ? Friend của con á.* (Why did your friend come over?)

LUCY *doesn't answer.* MUM *coughs.*

Con chỉ cần làm người tốt thôi là được rồi. Be good person. (You know, all you have to be is a good person.)

LUCY *starts to cry.*

Xung quanh mẹ ai cũng đạt được những điều họ muốn. Sang Tee thì có con trai học university, Ngô buy her new house at Ambient Estates. Mỗi lần mẹ qua nhà á, là lúc nào cũng khoe hết. Nhưng khoe được chút là lại cằn nhằn. Làm butcher thì mấy bữa nay bị supermarket lấn rồi. Con trai Tee thì come home late, đi đêm đi khuya ở đâu không biết. Rồi Ngô thì bị builder lừa mất seven thousand dollar, all gone. Mẹ phải ngồi đó nói với mấy bả, trời chị ơi, at least you're rich! Ít ra chị còn làm ăn được. Ít ra con trai chị học university. Nhưng con biết sao không. I never tell them about us. Mẹ chưa bao giờ kể là dad hay giúp mẹ làm trong garage sau khi tan ca, and we talk. Mẹ chưa bao giờ kể là lâu lâu mẹ cho con stay home when you not sick. I never tell them về cuộc sống của nhà mình. Con biết tại sao không? Không phải là vì mẹ ashamed. No. It is because some things are just good, this too good to be judged. (I see everyone around me getting the things they want in life. Sang Tee with her son at university, Ngo with her new house at Ambient Estates. And every time I go over to one of their houses, they always talk about it. But that proud talk soon turns into a list of complaints. The local butchering business is being seized by supermarkets these days. Tee's son comes home really late at night and she has no idea where he's been, Ngo's builder cheated them out of seven thousand dollars. And I have to sit there and tell them, well, sister, at least you're rich. At least you're successful. At least your boy is in university now. But do you know what I never do? I never tell them about us. I never tell them that your father often works in the garage with me after his shift and we talk. That I sometimes let you stay home with me when you're not sick. I never tell them about our lives. You know why? It is not because I am ashamed. It is because some things are just good, too good to be judged.)

> MUM *coughs.* MUM *continues to cough. She cannot stop—she can't get enough air in.*

LUCY: [*to* MUM] Hey Mum. Mum!

> MUM*'s breathing is raspy.*

Ba! Ba! Mum's not breathing. Dad!

DAD: *Mẹ con sao dợ? Mới nãy còn đang bình thường mà!* (What's wrong with her? She was fine moments ago.)

LUCY: Call the ambulance!

> DAD *calls 000.*
>
> *We see* MUM *helpless,* DAD *on the phone.*
>
> *Everything slows down.*
>
> LUCY *gets her mother up.* MUM *flinches, trying to get away. She starts to cough.*
>
> LUCY *holds her mother.*
>
> *The ambulance arrives. Paramedics put a facemask on* MUM. MUM *and* DAD *leave with paramedics.*
>
> *The sound of the sirens fading ...*

World morphs. CHELSEA *and* AMBER—*school yard.*

CHELSEA: The teachers think you're so innocent, with your sad brown eyes.

AMBER: We know. We know what you're like, you're devious.

CHELSEA: In some ways you are perfect for the Cabinet.

LUCY: Will you three just leave me alone? I'm done. I want out.

CHELSEA: So is your mum in a gang?

AMBER: The Cabinet doesn't associate with shady people.

CHELSEA: And you're not one of those—are you?

LUCY: What does that mean?

CHELSEA: You know what I'm talking about.

> LUCY *clocks the other students.*

LUCY: [*so the others can hear*] Why are you assuming I have any connection to the drug market?

AMBER: Do you?

LUCY: Piss off.

> *Silence.* LUCY *walks away. The crowd of girls 'ooohs'. No-one has ever been so brazen with the Cabinet before.*

AMBER: [*under her breath*] Go back to China, Chink.

> *Students 'oooh'.*

> *Time slows.* LINH *appears for the first time since the fight. They grab hands, turn to face the Cabinet together*

LUCY: You think growing up in Stanley I haven't heard it all before? What else you got? Chink, Gook, FOB, Chonky, Nip—well I've got some for you—bitch, cow, scrag—or do you need a more Laurindan vocabulary? Spiteful, malicious, callous, cruel. Don't look so fucking shocked. You do and say evil things every day and get away with it because you're the Cabinet. You bullied one of the kindest, smartest teachers out of this school and you broke Katie's hand!

> *A collective gasp from the students.*

If you were anywhere else you would have been suspended or expelled! I can't believe I felt special being part of your stupid group. You don't live in the real world! You're pampered, selfish, bitches.

LUCY / LINH: Fuck youse. Fuck youse.

A collective gasp. Jaws drop.

Yeah I know you can all hear me. And I don't give a shit. Fuck your Saturday sport. Fuck your debating. Fuck your extra fucking curricular activities. I'm not part of it. I'll never be part of it. You, you and you. You've used me to make yourselves look better. I came from a good school. I had great friends. I was happy.

Now, I'm in the newspaper every second week standing next to the principal. The local MP drops by, 'quick get Lucy for the photo-op'. I'm speaking at a conference to make white people feel good about how much 'good work' they're doing for multiculturalism! No-one ever asks me what I want. They don't care. I'm a puppet. A fucking puppet.

You are all sick. I am not your token TROPHY to show the world that you CARE. YOU DON'T FARKEN CARE ABOUT ANYONE BUT YOURSELVES. I am not one of youse. I am not a charity case. You make me SICK! The whole fucking lot of youse.

Beat.

FUCK YOUSE.

'Fuck youse' echoes as the school disappears and LINH *is gone again.* LUCY *crumples. Everything is empty. Silence.*

TULLY *appears.*

TULLY: Don't look at me like that. I don't need your pity Linh. You're out and I'm stuck—working in my parents' shitty shop for the rest of my life. Or I manage a good mark from a shitty school coz I work my arse off but then what? I have to work twice as hard, coz it matters where you go to school. It matters who you know. I was so close. One farking spot. All that work, study—gone to a selfish cow who didn't even want it. Fuck You.

CHARLOTTE: You used to be my favourite teacher but you are just like the rest of them.

The world spins.

A hospital, the present. MUM *is lying in the hospital bed.*

LUCY 37: Mum! Hey Mum? Is this real? Mum. I'm here. I bought your pajamas … and your toothbrush. You need a new toothbrush

Mum …

MUM *doesn't respond, she is sleeping.*

Those sedatives are working. Bruise looks like it's healing.

No more ambulance trips, okay? I can't take it. We're both too old for the stress. And you promised to tell me your secret ingredient in *cháo gà*. There's still so much … so many stories you haven't told me. I'm going to be around more. Why does everything feel … ?

You know, some of my students, they know what they want. And they don't care what anyone thinks.. With one video, or hashtag, they've called it out—cancelled it—one of them thinks I am a sellout … then … there are the ones who have so much to say, but can't, they don't know how to and I understand how hard it is for them to speak. It was my job to make it better. But I haven't. And my students think: 'Your generation didn't do enough', 'You didn't speak up, you didn't call bullshit.'

And they're right. I don't understand how today, a human being can be spat on, kicked and beaten and told to go back to where she came from. Well fuck youse you weak, spineless bastards. She's a human being. My mum. Quyen Lam.

LUCY 37 *puts her hand to her eye. It's twitching again. Beat.*

MUM: Toolly bought her mother an investment property.

LUCY 37: You're awake?

Beat.

MUM: *Hồi đó con bé, chắc con không nhớ, too young, lúc mình đang di tản on the boat, hải tặc Thái Lan, pirates, họ nhảy lên thuyền. Mới đầu mọi người tưởng là ngư dân đánh cá, nhưng sau đó thấy trên tay họ cầm knife. Bất chợt, bọn cướp đã ở trên thuyền mình, la hét ầm ĩ. Ba mẹ không hiểu bọn cướp nói gì, nhưng biết là phải quỳ xuống, úp bụng xuống sàn để họ lục người tìm vàng, find gold. Mẹ cứ quỳ, quỳ mãi. I had you flattened next to me and pray you don't cry. Even when there was silence, no one wanted to be the curious one. Hôm ấy chỉ có một người chết thôi;* the first to raise his head, dead. (You were too young to remember but when we were on the boat Thai pirates came. At first we thought they were fishermen, but then we saw the knives in their hands. Suddenly, they were on our boat, yelling. We couldn't understand them but we knew enough to get down on the deck and press our stomachs to the floor while they searched for any gold we might have. It seemed like time went on forever. I had you flattened next to me, and prayed that you would not start crying. Even when there was silence, no-one wanted to be the curious one. There was only one person killed that day, and he was the first to raise his head.)

LUCY 37: Be vigilant. Be silent.

MUM: We had to then, but you don't have to now.

> LUCY *is shocked back into 1997.*

LUCY: Dr Vanderwerp?

DR VANDERWERP: Lucy? Lucy Lam. Is that you?

LUCY: What are you doing in Stanley?

DR VANDERWERP: My father's house is just around the corner.

LUCY: Oh, I thought …

DR VANDERWERP: Are you alright?

> LUCY *weeps.*

LUCY: I was part of that awful class. They tormented you. I was a coward. I should have said something.

DR VANDERWERP: Lucy, you've been carrying this all this time? I wasn't in a good way back then.

> My father was in the hospital. I probably didn't handle things as well as I could have. I didn't leave because of a silly prank.

LUCY: I'm so sorry. I didn't know about your dad. My mum's in the hospital right now.

DR VANDERWERP: Is she going to be okay?

LUCY: I don't know. She isn't allowed to sew any more. We can't live on just Dad's wage. I don't know how to help.

DR VANDERWERP: Lucy, look at me. You are going to be okay. Whatever happens. Stanley breeds some pretty tough kids. I know. I was one.

LUCY: I'm so sorry about what we did to you.

DR VANDERWERP: I've been a teacher for a while, Lucy. I've taught in many schools—but I have never encountered anywhere quite like Laurinda. When I gave Brodie that B-plus … Brodie's mother went straight to Mrs Grey. They asked me to re-evaluate. I said no. But that disagreement was worth a fifty-thousand-dollar donation. And the girls sought their own retribution. So you see, Lucy—it was between them and me.

LUCY: Is your dad okay now?

DR VANDERWERP: He passed away.

LUCY *starts to tear up again.*

It's alright. He lived a long, full life and I got the gift of spending the last weeks of his life by his bedside.

Beat.

Lucy, I have wanted to ask you, why did you change your name when you came to Laurinda?

LUCY: I dunno.

DR VANDERWERP: Linh. It's a beautiful name. I looked up its etymology at the library.

LUCY: Yeah. Linh means soul.

A bell rings. School. The girls see LUCY *and whisper amongst themselves.*

KATIE: Lucy! It's so good to see you back. We—I—missed you. I can't believe you got suspended!

LUCY: I wasn't suspended.

KATIE: Of course you were. I saw you like go like off at the Cabinet. And the scholarship girl doesn't miss the last three days of term for no reason. Everyone like knows.

After you left, Mrs Grey told off Amber, Brodie and Chelsea. That never happens. They were pissed. I've never seen them so quiet. And Mrs Grey has like silenced Brodie!—She isn't allowed to speak at the Valedictory dinner now! It's like full on.

LUCY: What? Why would she tell them off?

KATIE: Because you like told everyone they broke my hand!

KATIE *laughs, hard.*

I mean you swore sooo much! I couldn't believe it. [*Whispering*] Fuck youse! Faarrrk youse!! It was like sooo great … You really put them in their place … those … bitches!

LUCY *goes to leave.*

You're not going to the library!

LUCY: I like it there.

KATIE: You know if you spend all your time in the library everyone is going to think you're like ashamed of yelling at the Cabinet.

LUCY: I don't care.

KATIE: Don't you get it Lucy? You stood up to them and now they're doing what they always do. Make up rumours. Making themselves the heroes. If they don't, it'll give other people ideas. We can fight this.

LUCY: / We?

KATIE: That's what friends do, right? No-one has ever stood up for me before. I can't let you go back to the library alone.

LUCY: I'm not alone.

KATIE: Unless you've got an imaginary friend Luce, you're alone.

> *In the classroom.*

CHELSEA: I have a photo of Dr Twerp's bum!

AMBER: Where did you manage to get a photo of his bum?

CHELSEA: At your birthday party. I thought it would be a good welcome back present!

BRODIE: Let me see that. Oh, my—

> *She giggles.*

That is a good angle.

AMBER: She was flirting so hard with Twerp. So gross.

> LUCY *looks at* KATIE.

KATIE: [*to* LUCY] Grab the photo!

> BRODIE *passes it back to* AMBER.

BRODIE: Touch me and it will be harassment.

> KATIE *lunges at* BRODIE.

> *The class gasps.*

> DR VANDERWERP *enters—there has been a shift in his energy.*

> *All the girls sit down.* CHELSEA *giggles.*

DR VANDERWERP: What is going on in here? What on earth are you doing?

> *Silence.* LUCY *stands up.*

LUCY: They have a photo of you from Amber's party. They took a photo of your backside.

KATIE: Amber / Leslie has it!

AMBER: I do not! How dare you Katie, you liar!

DR VANDERWERP: Okay ladies, that's enough.

AMBER: Sir, I would appreciate it if you stop looking at me like that. It's creeping me out.

DR VANDERWERP: Miss Leslie, give me the photograph.

> AMBER *turns out her books and folders.*

AMBER: You see, Sir? Nothing.

KATIE: Sir, it's in the inside pocket of her blazer.

CHELSEA: I don't understand why you're picking on Amber.

AMBER: Search me.

CHELSEA: Take it off for him Amber!

DR VANDERWERP: You stay right where you are, Amber Leslie!

CHELSEA: I'd be careful Dr Vanderwerp.

BRODIE: Last time it was a donation, this time it could be your job.

DR VANDERWERP: I do not appreciate threats, Miss Newberry.

> AMBER *smiles, takes her blazer off and whirls it above her head, joining* CHELSEA's *writhing.*

CHELSEA: What a sexy, sexy show! Shove it down your skirt, Amber! Let him find it.

> AMBER *does a dance with the photograph, provocatively putting it down her skirt, then continuing to dance.*

> LUCY *stands.*

KATIE: This isn't funny.

> *The Cabinet clap louder and begin to whoop.*

This is so stupid. Stop.

CHELSEA: Shut it Katie. Go cut yourself in a corner.

> *A collective gasp from the girls.*

TRISHA: Stop. This is mean.

> *All the students begin to stand.*

BRODIE: No-one wants to hear from you Trisha.

TRISHA: Well. I have something to say.

CHELSEA: I so can't wait to hear this.

TRISHA: I know this could make things worse. But I can't … Lucy … um … I just think …

DR VANDERWERP: Can everyone please / sit down.

TRISHA: Dr Vanderwerp—We've all stood by and we didn't say anything because we were scared and if history has taught us anything is that fear corrupts and we've all been corrupted.

CHELSEA: This isn't communist Russia!

TRISHA: No but we have been ruled by tyrants! I get it—when I play, I feel powerful and it is the best feeling in the world. But messing up his files so he's always confused, deliberately sneezing when we knew his dad was sick, spraying the classroom with deodorant, complaining about your marks, putting pigs' blood all over the desk and in his tea / is just mean.

DR VANDERWERP: Alright Trisha. Thank you.

TRISHA: Brodie, you don't need to do this, you already have so much. Amber, I'm sorry your mum doesn't give you the attention you need but I've seen you in orchestra. You could become a professional french horn player. And Chelsea, my parents are divorced too. It sux. But being mean to other people doesn't fix it.

I've been thinking about how brave Lucy was. We've all been so scared. But being scared—It's just not … fucking … good enough! We're better than this.

Beat.

All the students whoop and cheer.

LUCY *takes a moment, looks around and begins, for the first time in the play, to control the space.*

Lucy's parents help her change for the Valedictory dinner.

DAD: *Xin lỗi con, tối nay ba mẹ không đi Valedictory dinner của con được.* Sorry! (I'm sorry that we couldn't go with you tonight to the Valedictory dinner.)

MUM: *Mẹ mà đi thì phí luôn sixty-five dolla, tại mẹ sẽ không hiểu gì hết! No Englis!* (If I went, it would be a waste of sixty-five dollars. I wouldn't be able to understand anything.)

DAD: Do you know what you're going to say for your speech? This Valedictory speech is very important.

LUCY: I know Dad. Mrs Grey told me how important this is.

DAD: Very important.

LUCY: No pressure! I just want to do one thing this year that I am proud of.

MUM: Red. Lucky colour.

LUCY: I'll take all the luck I can get. *Cái đầm này đẹp quá mẹ. Thank you!* (The dress is great Mum. Thank you!)

DAD: *Nào, để ba chụp mấy bô ảnh coi. You look very beautiful tonight. And here, Linh.* (Come come. Let's me take some photos. You look very beautiful tonight. And here, Linh.)

> DAD *hands* LUCY *a small box. She opens it. It is a Nokia 3310.*

LUCY 37: Ha! Nokia. Vintage! Dad! We can't afford this. It's too much.

DAD: It nothing. Don't tell your mum. You worked hard this year. Okay. Okay.

> *The Valedictory dinner. Girls singing—*'Corncordia prosum, semper progrediens, semper sursum' [*'Forward harmony always progressing, always aiming high'*].

> *Applause.* LUCY *walks on stage.*

LUCY: [*reading her script*] Thank you for giving me the opportunity to speak this evening at the Valedictory dinner. My mum and dad are not here tonight, but their names are Warwick and Quyen Lam. When I was two, we came to Australia on a boat from Vietnam and settled in Stanley, one of the most socio-economically disadvantaged suburbs in Victoria.

LUCY 37: Linh! Do I have to do this again? I'd spent all year trying to figure out what was expected and I realised—If you looked the part you could play the part.

LINH: You were one smart teenager!

LUCY 37: Where have you been?!

LINH: Shhh. We're almost there. I was there then, so I'm here now.

> *Beat—*LINH *clears her throat.*

They're all waiting!

> LUCY *puts down the script.*

LUCY: If I could start this year again … I wouldn't. All year I haven't been able to turn my brain on because I was in survival mode. I couldn't keep up. I didn't know how to step up. I definitely didn't feel like leadership material. I wasn't 'always progressing. Always aiming high'. I just wanted to fit in. I've spent a lot of time this year watching and listening. I was noticing what was good and trying to keep myself grounded. You are not truly good until you are tested. And this year I have definitely been tested. And because of that, now, I feel like I *can* be a leader, because I know myself better and I'm not ashamed of where I come from.

LINH: That fifteen-year-old was not ashamed of where she came from.

LUCY 37: [*to* LINH] But she hasn't really come up against it yet, has she? She had no idea that she would meet people like the Cabinet everywhere, everywhere—holding power, silencing, setting the agenda.

LINH: What happened when the same obstacles you faced that year came up again and and again and again?

LUCY 37: You know what happened.

LINH: Say it.

LUCY 37: They wore me down. It slowly creeps up on you. You don't even realise that it's happening. All this time I've been doing what was expected of me. I've done everything 'right'. But got everything wrong.

LINH: Why, wrong?

LUCY 37: I haven't done enough. For my parents. For my students. For myself!

LINH: You did what you could in a world that wanted a poster girl while telling her to go back to where she came from.

LUCY 37: It was my job to make it better for the people who came after me.

LINH: You need to let that shit go.

LUCY: Isn't that the job?

LINH: Yeah but that's *their* job too.

LUCY: But I don't think they even know how!

LINH: Don't worry about them. You be you!

LUCY 37: I miss my fifteen-year-old self. I wish I still had some of that.

LINH: You are so thick. It's endearing but sad. We split. I'm *here*. Let me in. Please.

LUCY 37: What?

LINH: That's why we did all of this, because you needed to see it. That fifteen-year-old was almost there. But she hadn't put all the pieces together. Now it's time.

LINH *creates space and prepares for a run-up!*

LUCY 37: What are you doing?

LINH: You're ready now.

LUCY 37: Am I? For what?

LINH: You want some of that fifteen-year-old spirit? Lemme in.

LUCY 37: You mean inside?

LINH: Do I have your consent?

LUCY 37: I guess.

LINH: I need a clear yes or no.

LUCY 37: Yes?

LINH: Ready?

LUCY 37: Yes!

LINH *runs into* LUCY.

Ah fuck—

LUCY 37 / LINH: That hurt.

Silence.

LUCY 37: What just happened? Linh, Linh. Where did you go?

LINH: [*voiceover*] Feel better?

LINH *experiments in* LUCY*'s body again.* LUCY*'s arms fly up without her control. She does some funky dance moves.*

LUCY 37: Holy shit. Did it work?

LINH: [*voiceover*] Finally!

LUCY 37: But but / but

LINH: [*voiceover*] It was a great speech, I was standing beside you, but you never let me back in. Shame kept me out.

LUCY 37: Holy shit.

LUCY *does a little dance—and laughs with utter joy.*

LINH: Feels good, doesn't it?

LUCY 37: It does. It really does.

So what now?

LINH: [*voiceover*] Give me a hug.

LUCY 37: Seriously?

LINH: [*voiceover*] If you don't, I will.

    LUCY *takes her time to hug herself—a moment.*

    Silence.

    Silence.

LINH: [*voiceover*] Okay. You can let go now.

LUCY 37: Why am I crying?

LINH: [*voiceover*] Because you missed me.

    LUCY *starts to move.*

LUCY 37: Hang on? Where are we going?

LINH: [*voiceover*] We've got a speech to do, remember? And somehow. I don't think it's an accident that Brodie is presenting the award. Ready?

LUCY: Yeah. I am. Ready. Let's do this.

    Lights.

THE END

Fiona Choi in rehearsals for the Melbourne Theatre Company production of Laurinda. *Photo: Sarah Walker.*

Melbourne Theatre Company

BOARD OF MANAGEMENT
Jane Hansen AO (Chair)
Tony Burgess
Patricia Faulkner AO
Jonathan Feder
Larry Kamener
Professor Duncan Maskell
Susan Oliver AM
Leigh O'Neill
Professor Marie Sierra
Allan Tait
Anne-Louise Sarks
Virginia Lovett

FOUNDATION BOARD
Jonathan Feder (Chair)
Paul Bonnici
Jennifer Darbyshire
Shane Gild
Jane Grover
Hilary Scott
Tania Seary
Tracey Sisson
Virginia Lovett
Rob Pratt
Rupert Sherwood

EXECUTIVE MANAGEMENT
Artistic Director & Co-CEO
Anne-Louise Sarks
Executive Director & Co-CEO
Virginia Lovett
Executive Administrator
Emma Vincin
Executive Assistant to the Artistic Director & Co-CEO
Carmen Lai

ARTISTIC
Director of Artistic Operations/ Senior Producer
Martina Murray
Associate Director
Petra Kalive
Head of New Work
Jennifer Medway
Casting Director
Janine Snape
Casting Administrator
Carmen Lai
Associate Producer/ Senior Company Manager
Stephen Moore
Company Manager
Julia Smith
Programs Producer
Karin Farrell

DEVELOPMENT
Director of Development
Rupert Sherwood
Annual Giving Manager
Chris Walters
Major Gifts Manager
Sophie Boardley
Philanthropy Coordinator
Emily Jenik
Partnerships Manager
Portia Atkins
Partnerships Coordinator
Isobel Lake

EDUCATION
Head of Education & Families
Jeremy Rice
Learning Manager
Nick Tranter
Digital Content Producer
Bonnie Leigh-Dodds
First Peoples Young Artists Program Administrator & Schools Engagement Officer
Brodi Purtill

PEOPLE & CULTURE
Director of People & Culture
Sean Jameson
People & Culture Executive
Christine Verginis
Receptionist
David Zierk

FINANCE & IT
Director of Finance & IT
Rob Pratt
Finance Manager
Andrew Slee
IT & Systems Manager
Michael Schuettke
IT Support Officer
Darren Snowdon
Payroll Officer
Julia Godinho
Payments Officer
Harper St Clair
Assistant Accountant
Nicole Chong
Building Services Manager
Adrian Aderhold

MARKETING & COMMUNICATIONS
Marketing & Communications Director
Vanessa Rowsthorn
Marketing Manager
Rebecca Lawrence
Marketing Campaign Manager
Ashlee Read
Marketing Coordinator
Skylar Lin
Digital Engagement Manager
Jane Sutherland
Lead Graphic Designer/ Art Director
Kate Francis
Graphic Designer
Helena Turinski
Senior Manager, Communications & External Relations
Rosie Shepherdson-Cullen
Editorial Content Producer
Paige Farrell
Publicist
Wendy Trieu

TECHNICAL & PRODUCTION
Technical & Production Director
Adam J Howe

PRODUCTION
Senior Production Manager
Michele Preshaw
Production Manager
Jess Maguire
Production Assistant
Zsuzsa Gaynor Mihaly
Production Administrators
Alyson Brown
Michaela Deacon
Props Buyer/ SM Swing
Meg Richardson

TECHNICAL
Technical Manager
Kerry Saxby
Senior Production Technician Coordinator
Allan Hirons
Production Technician Coordinator
Nick Wollan
Production Technicians/Operators
Marcus Cook
Mungo Trumble
Bryn Cullen
Scott McAllister
Max Wilkie
Technical Manager – Staging & Design
Andrew Bellchambers
CAD Drafter
Jacob Battista
Head Mechanist
Michael Burnell

PROPERTIES
Properties Supervisor
Geoff McGregor
Props Maker
Colin Penn

SCENIC ART
Scenic Art Supervisor
Shane Dunn
Scenic Artist
Colin Harman
Alison Crawford

WORKSHOP
Workshop Supervisor
Andrew Weavers
Deputy Workshop Supervisor
Brian Easteal
Set Makers
Aldo Amenta
Ken Best
Nick Gray
Simon Juliff
Philip De Mulder
Peter Rosa

COSTUME
Costume Manager
Keryn Ribbands
Costume Staff
Jocelyn Creed
John Van Gastel
Lyn Molloy
Costume Coordinator
Sophie Woodward
Millinery
Phillip Rhodes
Wigs & Makeup
Jurga Celikiene
Costume Hire
Liz Symons
Costume Maintenance
Angela Silver

STAGE MANAGEMENT
Christine Bennett
Brittany Coombs
Lisette Drew
Jess Keepence
Whitney McNamara
Meg Richardson
Millie Mullinar
Vivienne Poznanski
Lucie Sutherland
Pippa Wright

SOUTHBANK THEATRE
Theatre Manager
Mark D Wheeler
Front of House Manager
James Cunningham
Events Manager
Mandy Jones
Production Services Manager
Frank Stoffels
Lighting Supervisor
Geoff Adams
Deputy Lighting Supervisor
Tom Roach
Sound Supervisor
Joy Weng
Fly Supervisor
James Tucker
Deputy Fly Supervisor
Adam Hanley
Stage & Technical Staff
Jon Bargen
Max Bowyer
Alice Brill
Suzanne Brown
Merlyn Brown
Sam Bruechert
Ash Buchanan
Emily Campbell
Steve Campbell
Will Campbell
Bryn Cullen
Kit Cunneen
Nathan Evers
Robert Harewood
Chris Hubbard
Julia Knibbs
Marcus Macris
Alexandre Malta
Terry McKibbin
David Membery
Maxwell Murray Lee
Will Paterson
James Paul
Jake Rogers
Jim Stenson
Max Wilkie
James Williams
Tom Willis
House Supervisors
Tanya Batt
Matt Bertram
Sarah Branton
Kasey Gambling
Daniel Moulds
Paul Terrell
Drew Thomson
House Attendants
George Abbott
Rhiannon Atkinson-Howatt
Stephanie Barham
Briannah Borg
Max Bowyer
Zak Brown
Sam Diamond
Ignacio Gasparini
Leila Gerges
Bear
Hugo Gutteridge
Michael Hart
Kathryn Joy
Natasha Milton
Ernesto Munoz
Ben Nichol
Rain Okpamen
Sam Perry
Taylor Reece
Adam Rogers
Sophie Scott
Mieke Singh
Olivia Walker
Alison Wheeldon

TICKETING
Director of Ticketing Operations
Brenna Sotiropoulos
Customer Service Sales Manager
Jessie Phillips
VIP Ticketing Officer
Michael Bingham
Education Ticketing Officer
Mellita Ilich
Subscriptions & Telemarketing Team Leader
Peter Dowd
Box Office Supervisors
Bridget Mackey
Daniel Scaffidi
Box Office Duty Supervisor
Tain Stangret
Box Office Attendants
Sarah Branton
Olivia Brewer
Britt Ferry
Darcy Fleming
Kasey Gambling
Min Kingham
Julia Landberg
Evan Lawson
Julie Leung
Debra McDougall
Lee Threadgold

CRM & AUDIENCE INSIGHTS
Director of CRM & Audience Insights
Jeremy Hodgins
Database Specialist
Ben Gu

COMMISSIONS
The Joan & Peter Clemenger Commissions
Kylie Coolwell
Anthony Weigh
NEXT STAGE Commissions
Van Badham
Carolyn Burns
Angus Cerini
Patricia Cornelius
Tim Finn
Elise Esther Hearst
Andrea James
Phillip Kavanagh
Anchuli Felicia King
Nathan Maynard
Diana Nguyen
Joe Penhall
Leah Purcell
Melissa Reeves
Chris Ryan
Megan Washington
Mark Leonard Winter

OVERSEAS REPRESENTATIVE
New York
Kevin Emrick

Circles of giving

MTC LIFETIME PATRONS
Acknowledging a lifetime of extraordinary support for MTC.

Pat Burke
Peter Clemenger AO and
Joan Clemenger AO

Greig Gailey and
Dr Geraldine Lazarus
Allan Myers AC QC and
Maria Myers AC

The Late Biddy Ponsford
The Late Dr Roger
Riordan AM
Maureen Wheeler AO and
Tony Wheeler AO

Ursula Whiteside
Caroline Young and
Derek Young AM

ENDOWMENT DONORS
Supporting the long term sustainability and creative future of MTC.

Leading Gifts
Jane Hansen AO and
Paul Little AO
The Late Max and Jill
Schultz
The University of
Melbourne

$50,000+
The Late Margaret
Anne Brien
Geoffrey Cohen AM
Orcadia Foundation
The Late Biddy Ponsford
Andrew Sisson AO and
Tracey Sisson
The John & Myriam Wylie
Foundation

$20,000+
Robert A. Dunster
Prof Margaret Gardner AO
and Prof Glyn Davis AC
Anne and Mark
Robertson OAM

$10,000+
Jane Kunstler
Anonymous

MTC'S PLAYWRIGHTS GIVING CIRCLE
Supporting the NEXT STAGE Writers' Program.

Louise Myer and Martyn Myer AO, Maureen Wheeler AO and Tony Wheeler AO, Christine Brown Bequest
Allan Myers AC QC and Maria Myers AC, Tony Burgess and Janine Burgess
Dr Andrew McAliece and Dr Richard Simmie, Larry Kamener and Petra Kamener

The Ian Potter Foundation — NAOMI MILGROM FOUNDATION — THE MYER FOUNDATION — MALCOLM ROBERTSON FOUNDATION — THE UNIVERSITY OF MELBOURNE

TRUSTS AND FOUNDATIONS

Besen Family FOUNDATION — BETTY AMSDEN FOUNDATION — Cybec Foundation — The Gailey Lazarus Foundation — HANSEN LITTLE FOUNDATION

The Ian Potter Foundation — JOHN & MYRIAM Wylie FOUNDATION — PLAYKING FOUNDATION — telematics trust — VICTORIA State Government — The Vizard FOUNDATION

Annual giving

Donors whose recent gifts help MTC enrich and transform lives through the finest theatre imaginable.

Acknowledging Donors who join together to support innovative and inspiring programs for the benefit of our community.

▲ ARTISTIC DIRECTORS ○ PRODUCTION PATRON ▣ YOUTH AMBASSADORS ◆ WOMEN IN THEATRE ● EDUCATION

BENEFACTORS CIRCLE

$50,000+
The Joan and Peter Clemenger Trust
Jane Hansen AO and Paul Little AO
Andrew Sisson AO and Tracey Sisson ○
Maureen Wheeler AO and Tony Wheeler AO

$20,000+
Paul & Wendy Bonnici and Family ●
Krystyna Campbell-Pretty AM ●
Greig Gailey and Dr Geraldine Lazarus
Louise and Martyn Myer AO
Janet Reid OAM and Allan Reid
Anne and Mark Robertson OAM ●
Orcadia Foundation ○

$10,000+
Joanna Baevski ○ ●
Erica Bagshaw ◆
Dr Jane Bird ◆
Jill Campbell ○
Kathleen Canfell ○
The Cattermole Family
Chelgrave Contracting Australia PTY LTD ○
Tom and Elana Cordiner ●
Jennifer Darbyshire and David Walker
Linda Herd ● ▣
Karen Inge and Dr George Janko
Petra and Larry Kamener
Daryl Kendrick and Sandy Bell
Suzanne Kirkham
Glenda and Greg Lewin AM ○
Macgeorge Bequest
Susanna Mason ▲
Ian and Margaret McKellar

McNeilly Family ○
George and Rosa Morstyn
Helen Nicolay ○
Lisa Ring
Craig Semple ○
Geoff Slade, Slade Group and TRANSEARCH ○
Rob Stewart and Lisa Dowd
Helen Sykes ○
Anita Ziemer ○
Anonymous (6)

$5,000+
John and Lorraine Bates
Marc Besen AC and Eva Besen AO
James Best and Doris Young
Jay Bethell and Peter Smart
Bill Bowness AO
Dr Andrew Buchanan and Peter Darcy
Ian and Jillian Buchanan
Bill Burdett AM and Sandra Burdett
Lynne and Rob Burgess
Pat Burke and Jan Nolan
Diana Burleigh
The Janet and Michael Buxton Foundation
Dr Anthony Dortimer and Jillian Dortimer
The Dowd Foundation
Prof Margaret Gardner AC and Prof Glyn Davis AC
Nigel and Cathy Garrard
Diana and Murray Gerstman
The Gjergja Family
Henry Gold

Robert and Jan Green
Lesley Griffin
John and Joan Grigg OAM
Jane Hemstritch
Tony Hillery and Warwick Eddington
Bruce and Mary Humphries
Amy and Paul Jasper
Marshall Day Acoustics (Dennis Irving Scholarship)
Dr Andrew McAliece and Dr Richard Simmie
Martin and Melissa McIntosh
Kim and Peter Monk ◆
Jane and Andrew Murray
Peter Nethercote – Ballarat Theatre Company
Tom and Ruth O'Dea ▣
Leigh O'Neill ◆
Dr Kia Pajouhesh (Smile Solutions)
Bruce Parncutt AO
Prof David Penington AC and Dr Sonay Hussein
Christopher Reed
Renzella Family
Lynne Sherwood
Tintagel Bay P/L
Trawalla Foundation Trust
The Veith Foundation
Ralph Ward-Ambler AM and Barbara Ward-Ambler
Marion Webster OAM ◆
Ursula Whiteside
Janet Whiting AM and Phil Lukies
J & M Wright Foundation
Anonymous (4)

ADVOCATES CIRCLE

$2,500+
Australian Communities Foundation – Ballandry (Peter Griffin Family) Fund
Ian Baker and Cheryl Saunders
Nan Brown
Jenny and Stephen Charles AO
Anne Cleary
Sandy and Yvonne Constantine
Ann Darby ○ ●
The Dodge Family Foundation
Rodney Dux
Dr Justin Friebel and Jessica Rose
Kerry Gardner AM and Andrew Myer AM
Gaye and John Gaylard
Heather and Bob Glindemann OAM
Roger and Jan Goldsmith
Fiona Griffiths and Tony Osmond ◆

Jane Grover ◆
Luke Heagerty
Jane Hodder ◆
Peter and Halina Jacobsen
Josephine and Graham Kraehe AO
Joan Lefroy AM and George Lefroy AM
Leg Up Foundation ▣
Lording Family Foundation
Virginia Lovett and Rose Hiscock ○
Prof Duncan Maskell
Don and Sue Matthews
Ging Muir and John McCawley ▣
Sandy and Sandra Murdoch
Luke and Janine Musgrave
Nelson Bros Funeral Services
Dr Paul Nisselle AM and Sue Nisselle
B & J Rollason
Scanlon Foundation

Hilary and Stuart Scott ●
In memory of Berek Segan AM OBE – Marysia & Marshall Segan ●
Prof Barry Sheehan and Pamela Waller
The Stobart Strauss Foundation
Ricci Swart AM
Richard and Debra Tegoni ● ◆
Anthony Watson and Tracey McDonald
Dr Peter and Dr Carole Wigg
Kaye and John de Wijn
Price and Christine Williams
The Ray and Margaret Wilson Foundation
Gillian and Tony Wood
Anonymous (8)

Annual giving

LOYALTY CIRCLE

$1,000+

Prof Noel Alpins AM and Sylvia Alpins
James Angus AO and Helen Angus
Mary-Louise Archibald
Margaret Astbury
Prof Robin Batterham
Sandra Beanham
Angelina Beninati
Tara Bishop ◆
Judy Bourke ●
Steve and Terry Bracks AM
Paul and Robyn Brasher
Brett Young Family
Bernadette Broberg
Nigel and Sheena Broughton
Dr Douglas and Treena Brown
Jannie Brown
Beth Brown and the late Tom Bruce AM
Julie Burke
Katie Burke
Hugh Burrill
Pam Caldwell
Alison and John Cameron
John and Jan Campbell
Jessica Canning
Clare and Richard Carlson
Fiona Caro
Chernov Family
Keith Chivers and Ron Peel
Assoc Prof Lyn Clearihan and
  Dr Anthony Palmer
Dr Robin Collier and Neil Collier
Deborah Conyngham ●
Karen and Rachel Cusack ◆
Ann Cutts
Mark and Jo Davey
Natasha Davies
Katharine Derham Moore
Sandra and Cameron Dorse
Robert Drake
Dr Sally Duguid and Dr David Tingay
Bev and Geoff Edwards
George and Eva Ermer
Anne Evans and Graham Evans AO
Dr Alastair Fearn
Melody and Jonathan Feder ▦
Grant Fisher and Helen Bird
Jan and Rob Flew
Rosemary Forbes and Ian Hocking
Bruce Freeman ▦
Glenn Fryer
John Fullerton
Gill Family Foundation

Charles and Cornelia Goode
  Foundation ◆
Ian and Wendy Haines
Charles Harkin
Mark and Jennifer Hayes ●
Diana Heggie ●
Kerri Hereward
Dr Alice Hill and Mark Nicholson
Howard and Glennys Hocking
Dr Romayne Holmes
Emeritus Prof Andrea Hull AO
Peter Jaffe and Judy Gold
Ben Johnson
Ed and Margaret Johnson
Sally and Rod Johnstone
K & B Jones
Leah Kaplan and Barry Levy
Irene Kearsey and Michael Ridley
Malcolm Kemp
Daniel Kilby
Anne and Terry King
Fiona Kirwan-Hamilton and
  Simon E Marks QC
Doris and Steve Klein
Marianne and Arthur Klepfisz
Larry Kornhauser and Natalya Gill ● ▦
Alan and Wendy Kozica
Anne Le Huray
Verona Lea
Alison Leslie
Peter and Judy Loney
Lord Family ◆
Kerryn Lowe and Raphael Arndt
Elizabeth Lyons
Chris and Bruce Maple
Ian and Judi Marshman
Margaret and John Mason OAM
Bernie and Virginia McIntosh
Heather and Simon McKeon ▦
Garry McLean
Libby McMeekin
Emeritus Prof Peter McPhee AM and
  Charlotte Allen
Melman Trading Pty Ltd
Robert and Helena Mestrovic
John G Millard
Ann Miller AM
Ross and Judy Milne-Pott
Patricia Montgomery
MK Futures
Barbara and David Mushin
Brian and Dianne Neilson
Sarah Nguyen
Nick Nichola and Ingrid Moyle

Michele and John Nielsen
David and Lisa Oertle
Susan Oliver AM
In loving memory of Richard Park
Dr Annamarie Perlesz
Peter Philpott and Robert Ratcliffe
Dug and Lisa Pomeroy
Catherine Quealy
Philip and Gayle Raftery
Sally Redlich
Victoria Redwood
Phillip Riggio
Ken Roche
Roslyn and Richard Rogers Family ●
Dr Paul and Gay Rosen
Paul Ross and Georgina Costello
Jeremy Ruskin and Roz Zalewski
Jenny Russo
Anne and Laurie Ryan
Edwina Sahhar
Margaret Sahhar AM
Lucy and Mathew Saliba
Elisabeth and Doug Scott
Fiona Scott
Sally and Tim Scott
Jacky and Rupert Sherwood
Diane Silk
Dr John Sime
Pauline and Tony Simioni
Jane Simon and Peter Cox
Tim and Angela Smith
Annette Smorgon ◆
Geoff Steinicke
Dr Ross and Helen Stillwell
Rosemary Stipanov
Helene Strawbridge
Suzy and Dr Mark Suss ▦
James and Anne Syme
Rodney and Aviva Taft
Megan and Damian Thomson
John and Anna van Weel
Valeria Vanselow
Fiona Viney
Graham Wademan and
  Michael Bowden
Walter and Gertie Wagner ●
Kevin and Elizabeth Walsh ▦
Pinky Watson
Penelope and Joshua White
Ann and Alan Wilkinson ●
Mandy and Edward Yencken
Graeme and Nancy Yeomans
Anonymous (53)

LEGACY CIRCLE

Acknowledging supporters who have made the visionary gesture of including a gift to MTC in their will.

John and Lorraine Bates
Mark and Tamara Boldiston
Bernadette Broberg
Adam and Donna Cusack-Muller
Peter and Betty Game

Fiona Griffiths
Linda Herd
Irene Kearsey
Dr Andrew McAliece and
  Dr Richard Simmie

Libby McMeekin
Peter Philpott and Robert Ratcliffe
Jillian Smith
Diane Tweeddale
Anonymous (14)

Thank you

MTC would like to thank the following organisations for their generous support.

Major Partners

Forum Night & MTC Digital Theatre Partner

ANZ

Future Directors Initiative Partner

MinterEllison.

Major Marketing Partners

ooh!
unmissable

The Monthly
The Saturday Paper
7am

Presenting Partners

Genovese

THE LANGHAM
MELBOURNE

LITTLE
GROUP

Associate Partners

AEGEUS

Frontier
software
Human Capital Management
& Payroll Software/Services

K&L GATES

Supporting Partners

THE LUXURY NETWORK

METROPOLIS
EVENTS

QUEST
SOUTHBANK

SOH
MELBOURNE

SUPERNORMAL
スーパー・ノーマル

taxi kitchen

Wilson Parking

Marketing Partners

BROADSHEET

CINEMA NOVA

invicium
print and beyond

southgate

3RRR

Southbank Theatre Partners

CHANDON

mgc
THE MELBOURNE GIN COMPANY

SCOTCHMANS HILL
BELLARINE PENINSULA
VICTORIA
ESTABLISHED 1982

Current as of June 2022. To learn more about partnership opportunities at MTC or to host a private event, please contact **partnerships@mtc.com.au**

www.ingramcontent.com/pod-product-compliance
Lightning Source LLC
Chambersburg PA
CBHW050021090426
42734CB00021B/3363